THE COLLECTED POEMS
OF ISAAC ROSENBERG

THE COLLECTED POEMS OF
ISAAC ROSENBERG

Edited by
GORDON BOTTOMLEY & DENYS HARDING

With a Foreword by
SIEGFRIED SASSOON

SCHOCKEN BOOKS/NEW YORK

Published in U.S.A. in 1949
by Schocken Books Inc.
200 Madison Avenue, New York, N.Y. 10016

Foreword © The Executors of Siegfried Sassoon 1937
Editorial Matter, Selection and Arrangement © Denys Harding
and Gordon Bottomley 1937
Poems marked © at the foot of page are Copyright
The Literary Executors of Mrs. A. Wynick, 1937

Library of Congress Catalog Card No. 73–91125

Second Printing 1974

Printed in Great Britain

Contents

FOREWORD

IT has been considered appropriate that I should say some-
thing about the poems of Isaac Rosenberg. I can only
hope that what I say, inadequate though it may be, will help
to gain for him the full recognition of his genius which has
hitherto been delayed. In reading and re-reading these
poems I have been strongly impressed by their depth and
integrity. I have found a sensitive and vigorous mind
energetically interested in experimenting with language, and
I have recognised in Rosenberg a fruitful fusion between
English and Hebrew culture. Behind all his poetry there
is a racial quality—biblical and prophetic. Scriptural and
sculptural are the epithets I would apply to him. His
experiments were a strenuous effort for impassioned ex-
pression; his imagination had a sinewy and muscular alive-
ness; often he saw things in terms of sculpture, but he did
not carve or chisel; he *modelled* words with fierce energy
and aspiration, finding ecstasy in form, dreaming in grandeurs
of superb light and deep shadow; his poetic visions are
mostly in sombre colours and looming sculptural masses,
molten and amply wrought. Watching him working with
words, I find him a poet of movement; words which express
movement are often used by him and are essential to his
natural utterance.

Rosenberg was not consciously a 'war poet'. But the
war destroyed him, and his few but impressive 'Trench
Poems' are a central point in this book. They have the
controlled directness of a man finding his true voice and
achieving mastery of his material; words and images obey
him, instead of leading him into over-elaboration. They
are all of them fine poems, but 'Break of Day in the Trenches'
has for me a poignant and nostalgic quality which eliminates
critical analysis. Sensuous front-line existence is there,
hateful and repellent, unforgettable and inescapable. And
beyond this poem I see the poems he might have written
after the war, and the life he might have lived when life

vii

began again beyond and behind those trenches which were the limbo of all sane humanity and world-improving imagination. For the spirit of poetry looks beyond life's trench-lines. And Isaac Rosenberg was naturally empowered with something of the divine spirit which touches our human clay to sublimity of expression.

Here, in this book, we have his immaturity and his achievement. Both are wonderful and manifold in richness. Having said what I can, I lay this reverent wreath upon his tomb.

SIEGFRIED SASSOON

BIOGRAPHICAL NOTE

ISAAC ROSENBERG was born on November 25th, 1890, at Bristol. In 1897 his family came to London and he attended elementary schools in Stepney until he was fourteen. He was then apprenticed as an engraver in a firm of 'art publishers' and went to classes at the Art School of Birkbeck College in the evenings. He wanted to make painting his career, and in 1911, some time after his apprenticeship was over, three ladies (Mrs Delissa Joseph, Mrs E. D. Lowy, and Mrs Herbert Cohen) provided the means for his training at the Slade School.

He continued to write poetry (he had begun when he was very young) and with the help and encouragement of his sister, now Mrs I. Wynick, he circulated copies of his poems, winning the friendly interest of a number of writers and critics. In 1912 he published a pamphlet of poetry, the first of three that he had printed at his own expense. Neither his poetry nor his painting secured him any appreciable success materially. In 1914 he was told that his lungs were weak, and he therefore went to South Africa where another of his sisters was living. He came back to England in 1915, and after a time enlisted in the army. Early in 1916 he was sent to France, and on April 1st, 1918, he was killed in action.

EDITORIAL NOTE

APART from a few pieces of work which came out in periodicals Rosenberg's only publications during his life were the following three pamphlets, published at his own expense:

Night and Day, by Isaac Rosenberg. [1912.] Pp. 24.

Youth, by Isaac Rosenberg. London, I. Narodiczky, Printer, 48 Mile End Road, E. 1915. Pp. 18.

Moses. A Play, by Isaac Rosenberg. London, Printed by the Paragon Printing Works, 8 Ocean Street, Stepney Green, E. 1916. Pp. ii + 26.

After Rosenberg's death the task of bringing out a volume of his poetry was undertaken by Gordon Bottomley. Commercial exigencies restricted the size of this book, but it contained the greater part of his finished poetry and appeared as—

Poems, by Isaac Rosenberg, selected and edited by Gordon Bottomley, with an introductory memoir by Laurence Binyon. London, William Heinemann. 1922. Pp. xii + 188, with portrait.

For the present edition the work of collating the sources and preparing the material for press has been carried out by Denys Harding in consultation with Gordon Bottomley. A number of the poems have been preserved solely through their inclusion in Poems (1922) or in typescript copies made by Gordon Bottomley when that volume was in preparation; for the remainder of the work the sources have been Rosenberg's manuscripts, typescripts made for him during his lifetime, and the pamphlets which he published.

The material has here been arranged according to the following plan. The contents of the three pamphlets come first, in chronological order, followed by the remaining war poems, also in chronological order, and 'The Unicorn'. Then come earlier poems which were not printed by Rosenberg, these being arranged in inverse chronological order. Where a date is given there is fairly conclusive external evidence for it; in other cases there has sometimes been external evidence to suggest the date roughly

I

and sometimes only the internal evidence of style, recurrent phrases, etc., upon which to base a judgment.

Amongst the Fragments there have been included a small number of completed poems which seem to have been doggerel composed for social occasions. This material also is arranged in inverse chronological order so far as that could be discovered. All the available fragments of Rosenberg's work are given here with the exception of one or two of the very roughest jottings which convey next to nothing. Early versions of work for which there is also a revised version have not been included.

In including all the existing material the editors recognise that they are publishing much which Rosenberg would have destroyed or recast had he lived. They do so in the belief that many readers who already appreciate Rosenberg's achievement will prefer to form their own conception of his developing personality rather than to accept an impression conveyed by selective editing.

The spelling has been corrected, and errors of grammar have been removed except in a few instances where their removal would have appreciably altered Rosenberg's idiom. Rosenberg gave little attention to punctuation, and his frequent but quite unsystematic omissions and irregularities would have been only a source of distraction if they had been preserved. A few changes of punctuation, sufficient merely to prevent this distraction in reading, have therefore been made. In general only the comma and the full stop have been used, these being the points Rosenberg himself chiefly relied upon.

The Editors are greatly indebted to the many friends and associates of Rosenberg who have preserved his work and made it available for this edition; and especially to the poet's sister, Mrs I. Wynick. Finally they wish to record their appreciation of the great help given them by the publishers, and of the care and patience exercised by the printers in carrying out what was in some respects an unusual task.

NIGHT AND DAY

1912

NIGHT AND DAY

ARGUMENT

NIGHT. The Poet wanders through the night and questions
of the stars but receives no answer. He walks through
the crowds of the streets, and asks himself whether he is
the scapegoat to bear the sins of humanity upon himself,
and to waste his life to discover the secret of God, for all.
DAY. He wakes, and sees the day through his window. He
feels endowed with a larger capacity to feel and enjoy
things, and knows that by having communed with the
stars, his soul has exalted itself, and become wiser in
intellectual experience. He walks through the city, out
into the woods, and lies under the trees, dreaming through
the sky-spaces.

He hears Desire sing a song of immortality,
Hope, a song of love,
And Beauty, a song of the Eternal rhythm.

Twilight comes down and the poet hearkens to the
song of the evening star, for Beauty has taught him to
hear, Hope to feel, and Desire, a conception of attainment.

By thinking of higher things we exalt ourselves to
what we think about.

Striving after the perfect—God, we attain nearer to
perfection than before.

NIGHT

When the night is warm with wings
Invisible, articulate,
Only the wind sings
To our mortal ears of fault.
And the steadfast eyes of fate
Gleam from Heaven's brooding vault,
Through dull corporeal bars
We drink in the proud stars.

5

These, my earth-sundered fantasy
On pillared heights of thought doth see
In the dark heaven as golden pendulous
    birds,
Whose tremulous wings the wind trans-
    slates to words,
From the thrilled heaven which is their
    rapturous nest.
Still, though they sleep not, thoughtful
    to illume,
They are not silent, only our sundering
    gloom
Makes their songs dumb to us—a tragic
    jest.

Sing to me, for my soul's eyes
Anguish for these ecstasies
And voluptuous mysteries
That must somewhere be,
Or we could not know of them.
Sing to me, O sing to me,
Is your light from sun of them,
Or from boughs of golden stem
Trickling over ye,
That your nest is hanging on?

Though the sun's face be on high,
Yet his fiery feet do lie
Fixed on earth, to give the sky
In our hands a while.
So our mortal hearts make bliss,
And we may a little smile.
Wherefore keep ye all your bliss?
What your gain for gain we miss?

Wherefore so beguile
With your shining, heard of none?

6

How can I burst this trammel of my flesh,
That is a continent 'twixt your song and
    me?
How can I loosen from my soul this mesh
That dulls mine ears and blinds mine
    eyes to see?

When I had clambered over the walls of
    night,
Lo! still the night lay unperturb'd behind.
Only in Heaven the starry birds of light
Swarmed as arrested in their showery flight.
O! could I bind your song as night can
    bind.

.   .   .   .   .

Sudden the night blazed open at my feet.
Like splintered crystal tangled with gold
    dust
Blared on my ear and eye the populous
    street.

Then, like a dark globe sprinkled with
    gold heat
Wherein dark waters move—dark gleaming
    seas,
So round the lit-faced shadows seemed the
    street.

They feel the skeleton rattle as they go,
'Let us forget', they cry, 'soon we shall
    know,—
Drown in life's carnival fate's whisperings.'

Foul heat of painted faces, ribald breath,
Lewd leer, make up the pageant as they flow
In reeking passage to the house of death.

Then said I, what divides love's name
    from lust?
Behold, what word can name the life for
    these?
For starven and not hungered, O! what
    crust?
Lean—starven, and they hunger not in-
    crease.
Starven of light, barriered 'gainst purity,
A bruten lust of living their life's lease.

A dream-empearled ladder to the moon,
A thought-enguarded heavenly embassy
To treat with God for a perpetual June,

Colours my youth's flower for them, for
    me.
One flower whose ardent fragrance wastes
    for all.
Fed with the sobbings of humanity.

The sobbing of the burden of their sins
Is all the guerdon strife to ease them wins.
Who seeks heaven's sign, earth's scape-
    goat must he be?

God gives no June, and Heaven is a wall.
No symboled answer to my questionings—
Only the weak wind yearns, the stars wink
    not at all.

DAY

The fiery hoofs of day have trampled the
    night to dust;
They have broken the censer of darkness
    and its fumes are lost in light.
Like a smoke blown away by the rushing
    of the gust
When the doors of the sun flung open,
    morning leaped and smote the night.

The banners of the day flame from the east.
Its gorgeous hosts assail the heart of dreams.
They brush aside the strange and cowled
    priest
Who ministers to our pillows with moon-
    beams
And restful pageantry or lethe draught,
Sleep—who by day dwells in invisibleness—
Their noising stirs the waking veils of
    thought,
Ah! I am in the midst of their bright press.

I went to sleep in the night,
In the awed and shadowy night,
Pleading of those birds delight.
Where has the morning borne me to?
What has she done with the night?
And those birds flown whereto?

Surely some God hath breathed upon mine
    eyes
Between awake and waking, or poured
    strange wine
Of some large knowledge—for I am grown
    wise
And big with new life—eager and divine.

9

Last night I stripped my soul of all alloy
Of earth that did ensphere and fetter it.
I strove to touch the springs of all the night.
My brow felt spray, but hands and eyes
    were dry.

Last night my soul thought God—my soul
    felt God.
I prayed the stars this for my body's dole.
Through prayer and thought to purified
    desires.
Through hallowed thought I was made half
    divine.

Shall I dream of shadow
Now I have the light:
Spoil the sunny meadow
To think of night?

Forth into the woods I will fare.
I will walk through the great clanging city
To seek what all have sought to find.
No face shall pass me
But I will question therein
Some mirrored subtlety,
Some wandering gleam that straggled
    through
Nativity, from the forgotten shelter of
    God's skirts.
In all that Time has harvested,
Whether a seed from Heaven has sprung:
In all God has made mutable and swift
Some lustre of his smile to see.
And the dun monstrous buildings be a book
To read the malediction of lucre
That spreads a shade and shelter for a plague.

Noon blazes in the city, tumult whirled.

Flame crowned and garmented
With robes that flaunt
The splash of gold he throws
About my feet,
He weaves above my head
A golden chaunt,
A song that throbs and glows
Through all the noon-day heat.

No Pan-pipe melodies
Of wind and boughs.
No tired wave's listless wash:
No silence deep
With spirit harmonies
Night only knows;
No tender breaking flush,
Dawn's voice of dream-asleep.

But buildings glorified,
Whose windows shine
And show the heaven, while far
Down the throng'd street
Mingles man's song of pride
With the divine
Song of the day's great star
Struck from the noon-day heat.

.   .   .   .

Shall I turn me to this tavern
And so rest me from the sultriness?

.   .   .   .   .

Dim-watery-lights, gleaming on gibbering
    faces,

Faces speechful, barren of soul and sordid.
Huddled and chewing a jest, lewd and
    gabbled insidious.
Laughter born of its dung, flashes and floods
    like sunlight
Filling the room with a sense of a soul leth-
    argic and kindly,
Touches my soul with a pathos, a hint of a
    wide desolation.

.   .   .   .   .

Green foliage kisses my heart's sight
Before I yet have left the street,
My heart feels summer-leaping light
These summer silent guests to greet.
The grassy plot with rows of trees,
Like some sweet pallisaded land
From off some land outcast of these,
Whose air you breathe is grinding sand.

These are the outskirts of the woods,
The shore of mighty forest seas,
Where Pan plays to the solitudes
His deep primordial melodies.
Where night and day like ships sail by,
And no man knoweth this miracle;
Eternal as the eternal sky
That is the earth's dumb oracle.

.   .   .   .

I saw the face of God to-day,
I heard the music of his smile,
And yet I was not far away,
And yet in Paradise the while.

I lay upon the sparkling grass,
And God's own mouth was kissing me.

And there was nothing that did pass
But blazèd with divinity.

Divine—divine—upon my eyes,
Upon my hair—divine—divine,
The fervour of the golden skies,
The ardent gaze of God on mine.

Let me weave my fantasy
Of this web like broken glass
Gleaming through the fretted leaves
In quaint intricacy,
Diamond tipping all the grass.

Hearken as the spirit heaves
Through the branches and the leaves
In the shudder of their pulse;
Delicate nature trembles so
To a ruder nature's touch;
And of peace that these convulse
They have little who should have much.
Life is so.
Let me carve my fantasy
Of the fretwork of the leaves.

Then the trees bent and shook with laughter
Each leaf sparkled and danced with glee.
On my heart their sobs came after,
Demons gurgling over me.
And my heart was chilled and shaken,
And I said through my great fear,
When the throat of tears is slaken
Joy must come for joy will hear.

Then spake I to the tree,
Were ye your own desire
What is it ye would be?

Answered the tree to me,
'I am my own desire;
I am what I would be.

'If ye were your desire
Would ye lie under me,
And see me as you see?'

I am my own desire
While I lie under you,
And that which I would be
Desire will sing to you.

Through the web of broken glass
I knew her eyes looked on me.
Soon through all the leaves did pass
Her trembling melody.
Yea! even the life within the grass
Made green stir
So to hear
Desire's yearned song of immortality.

'Mortals—ancient syllables
Spoken of God's mouth,—
Lo! what spirits chronicle
So they be not lost?

'Music, breathed ephemeral—
Fragrant maid and child:
Bellow, croak and droning—
Age and cumbrous man.

'Music that the croaking hears:
Croak, to mate the music:
Lo! Angels stand and throw their nets
For you, from banks Eterne?'

'Surely the speech of God's mouth
Shall not be for naught!
Music wrought of God's passion
Less than vanished dew?

'As the sea through cloud to sea,
Thought through deed to thought,
Each returneth as they were,
So man to God's mouth?'

So man to God's mouth,
Mouth whose breath we are!
How far—O—how far!
Spring of the soul's drouth?

I heard a whisper once
Of a way to make it near,
And still that whisper haunts
Like a wonder round my ear.

Hope whispered to me,—
I could not hear
The meaning to subdue me
Of the music most clear.

.   .   .   .

'Music that the croaking hears,
Croak, to mate the music.'
Was it lorn Echo babbling to herself,
That none would mate and none would hear her?

'I wander—I wander—O will she wander here?
Where'er my footsteps carry me I know that she
    is near.

A jewelled lamp within her hand and jewels in
    her hair,
I lost her in a vision once and seek her every-
    where.

'My spirit whispers she is near, I look at you and
    you.
Surely she has not passed me, I sleeping as she
    flew.
I wander—I wander, and yet she is not here,
Although my spirit whispers to me that she is
    near.'

Verily my heart doth know the voice of Hope.
What doth he in these woods singing this wise?

'By what far ways shall my heart reach to thine?
We, who have never parted—never met,
Nor done to death the joys that shall be yet,
Nor drained the cup of love's delirious wine.
How shall my craving spirit know for mine
Thine, self-same seeking? Will a wild regret
For the lost days—the lonely suns that set,
Be for our love a token and a sign?
Will all the weary nights, the widowed days
That, sundered long, all point their hands at thee?
Yea! all the stars that have not heard thy praise
Low murmur in thy charmèd ear of me?
All pointing to the ending of the ways,
All singing of the love that is to be?'

Of love to be, wherefore of love to be?
I never have heard the stars though they look
    wistfully at me.
I have cried to them and they showed me Desire.
She brought me a passionate wistful dream of
    eternity.

I cried to them, and they showed me Hope—a
    fire.
He brought me a dream of love—he made my
    heart to feel

Vague shadowy longings—whereon loneliness
    had put a seal.
Wherefore? because love is the radiant smile of
    God,
Because love's land is a heaven only by angels
    trod.
Where beauty sings and teaches her fair song
Of the Eternal rhythm—ah! teach me.

'Close thine eyes and under the eyelids that hide,
The glory thine eyes have seen in thy soul shall
    abide.
The beauty thy soul has heard shall flow into
    thy soul.
Lordship of many mysteries will be thine being
    beauty's thrall.

'Close thine eyes and under the eyelids that hide
A bridge build from Heaven as the earth is—
    wide,
For the bright and dense shapes that 'twixt earth
    and heaven do pass,
Lutanists of day and even to the pool and to the
    grass.

'To the cloud and to the mountains, to the wind
    and to the stars,
Silvern tonguèd din of fountains, golden at the
    sunset bars.

'So they sing the songs I taught them, and they
    lute the songs I made
For the praise of Him who wrought them lauders
    of his sun and shade.

'How may there be a silence? for the cosmic cycle
    would cease,
I am but the voice of God and these do lute
    my litanies.'

  .   .   .   .   .   .

One night and one day and what sang Desire?
All that God sings betwixt them is not lost.
One night and one day, what did Beauty choir?
If our souls hearken little is the most,
And nothing is which is not living sound,
All flowing with the eternal harmony
That with creation's first day was unwound.
One night and one day—what sang Hope to me?
That the next night and day love's song must fill.
He showed me in a mirror, ecstasy,
And a new dawn break over the old hill.

Twilight's wide eyes are mystical
With some far off knowledge,
Secret is the mouth of her,
And secret her eyes.

Lo! she braideth her hair
Of dim soft purple and thread of satin.
Lo! she flasheth her hand—
Her hand of pearl and silver in shadow.
Slowly she braideth her hair
Over her glimmering eyes,
Floating her ambient robes
Over the trees and the skies,
Over the wind-footing grass.

Softly she braideth her hair
With shadow deeper than thought.

To make her comely for night?
To make her meet for the night?
Slowly she heaveth her breast,
For the night to lie there and rest?

Hush, her eyes are in trance
Swooningly raised to the sky.
What heareth she so to enthral?
Filleth her sight to amaze?

'From the sweet gardens of the sky
Whose roots are pleasures under earth,
Whose atmosphere is melody
To hail each deathless minute's birth,
Between frail night and frailer day
I sing what soon the moon will say,
And what the sun has said in mirth.

'I sing the centre of all bliss.
The peace like a sweet-smelling tree
That spreads its perfumed holiness
In unperturbed serenity.
Between the darkness and the light,
I hang above my message bright
The clamour of mortality.

'Here, from the bowers of Paradise
Whose flowers from deep contentment grew,
To reach his hand out to the wise
My casement God's bright eyes look through.
For him whose eyes do look for Him
He leans out through the seraphim
And His own bosom draws him to.'

I heard the evening star.

ASPIRATION *

The roots of a dead universe are shrunken in my brain;
And the tinsel leafèd branches of the charred trees are
    strewn;
And the chaff we deem'd for harvest shall be turned to
    golden grain,
While May no more will mimic March, but June be only
    June.

Lo! a ghost enleaguer'd city where no ghostly footfall
    came!
And a rose within the mirror with the fragrance of it hid;
And mine ear prest to the mouth of the shadow of a name;
But no ghost or speech or fragrance breathing on my faint
    eyelid.

I would crash the city's ramparts, touch the ghostly hands
    without.
Break the mirror, feel the scented warm lit petals of the
    rose.
Would mine ears be stretched for shadows in the fading
    of the doubt?
Other ears shall wait my shadow,—can you see behind
    the brows?

For I would see with mine own eyes the glory and the
    gold.
With a strange and fervid vision see the glamour and the
    dream.
And chant an incantation in a measure new and bold,
And enaureole a glory round an unawakened theme.

TO J. H. AMSCHEWITZ   *

In the wide darkness of the shade of days
Twixt days that were and days that yet will be,
Making the days that are gloom'd mystery,
What starshine glimmers through the nighted ways
Uplifting? and through all vain hope's delays
What is it brings far joy's foretaste to me?
A savour of a ship unsullied sea,
A glimpse of golden lands too high for praise.

Life holds the glass but gives us tears for wine.
But if at times he changes in his hand
The bitter goblet for the drink divine,
I stand upon the shore of a strange land.
And when mine eyes unblinded of the brine
See clear, lo! where he stood before, you stand.

HEART'S FIRST WORD

[I]

To sweeten a swift minute so
With such rare fragrance of sweet
    speech,
And make the after hours go
In a blank yearning each on each;
To drain the springs till they be dry,
And then in anguish thirst for drink,
So but to glimpse her robe thirst I,
And my soul hungers and I sink.

There is no word that we have said
Whereby the lips and heart are fire;
No look the linkèd glances read
That held the springs of deep desire.
And yet the sounds her glad lips gave
Are on my soul vibrating still.
Her eyes that swept me as a wave
Shine my soul's worship to fulfil.

Her hair, her eyes, her throat and chin;
Sweet hair, sweet eyes, sweet throat, so
    sweet,
So fair because the ways of sin
Have never known her perfect feet.
By what far ways and marvellous
May I such lovely heaven reach?
What dread dark seas and perilous
Lie 'twixt love's silence and love's
    speech?

'WHEN I WENT FORTH' *

When I went forth as is my daily wont
Into the streets, into the eddying throng,
Lady—the thought of your sweet face was strong,
The grace of your sweet shape my ways did haunt.
About this spell clangoured the busy chaunt
Of traffic, like some hundred-throated song
Of storm set round some moon-flashed isle in wrong.
But soon usurped your robes' undulant flaunt—
Your last words said—your ruby gaolers' loss—
The instant and unanchored gleams across
My soul's mirror that holds you there for aye;
The sounds that beat the guard down of sound's gates,
But memory mastereth not, behind who waits,
Your speech—your face—his text by night and day.

IN NOVEMBER *

Your face was like a day in June
Glad with the raiment of the noon,
And your eyes seemed like thoughts that
    stir
To dream of warm June nights that were.

The dead leaves dropped off one by one,
All hopeless in the withered sun.
Around, the listless atmosphere
Hung grey and quiet and austere.

As we stood talking in the porch
My pulse shook like a wind kissed torch,
Too sweet you seemed for anything
Save dreams whereof the poets sing.

Your voice was like the buds that burst
With latter spring to slake their thirst,
While all your ardent mouth was lit
With summer memories exquisite.

'LADY, YOU ARE MY GOD'

Lady, you are my God—
Lady, you are my heaven.

If I am your God
Labour for your heaven.

Lady, you are my God,
And shall not love win heaven?

If Love made me God
Deeds must win my heaven.

If my love made you God
What more can I for heaven?

SPIRITUAL ISOLATION

Fragment

My Maker shunneth me.
Even as a wretch stricken with leprosy
So hold I pestilent supremacy.
Yea! He hath fled as far as the uttermost star,
Beyond the unperturbèd fastnesses of night,
And dreams that bastioned are
By fretted towers of sleep that scare His light.

Of wisdom writ, whereto
My burdened feet may best withouten rue,
I may not spell—and I am sore to do.
Yea! all seeing my Maker hath such dread,
Even mine own self-love wists not but to fly
To Him, and sore besped
Leaves me, its captain, in such mutiny.

Will, deemed incorporate,
With me, hath flown ere love, to expiate
Its sinful stay where he did habitate.
Ah me! if they had left a sepulchre;
But no—the light hath changed not and in it
Of its same colour stir
Spirits I see not but phantasm'd feel to flit.

Air legioned such stirreth,
So that I seem to draw them with my breath.
Ghouls that devour each joy they do to death.
Strange glimmering griefs and sorrowing
        silences,
Bearing dead flowers unseen whose charnel
        smell
Great awe to my sense is
Even in the rose time when all else is well.

In my great loneliness,
This haunted desolation's dire distress,
I strove with April buds my thoughts to dress,
Therewith to reach to joy through gay attire;
But as I plucked came one of those pale griefs
With mouth of parched desire
And breathed upon the buds and charred the leaves.

TESS

The free fair life that has never been mine, the glory that
    might have been,
If I were what you seem to be and what I may not be!
I know I walk upon the earth but a dreadful wall between
My spirit and your spirit lies, your joy and my misery.

The angels that lie watching us, the little human play—
What deem they of the laughter and the tears that flow
    apart?
When a word of man is a woman's doom do they turn
    and wonder and say,
'Ah, why has God made love so great that love must
    burst her heart?'

'O! IN A WORLD OF MEN AND WOMEN'

O! in a world of men and women
Where all things seemed so strange to me,
And speech the common world called human
For me was a vain mimicry,

I thought—O! am I one in sorrow?
Or is the world more quick to hide
Their pain with raiment that they borrow
From pleasure in the house of pride?

O! joy of mine, O! longed for stranger,
How I would greet you if you came!
In the world's joys I've been a ranger,
In my world sorrow is their name.

YOUTH
1915

NONE HAVE SEEN THE LORD OF THE HOUSE *

Stealth-hushed, the coiled night
    nesteth
In woods where light has strayed;
She is the shadow of the soul—
A virgin and afraid,
That in the absent Sultan's chamber
    resteth,
Sleepless for fear he call.

Lord of this moon-dim mansion,
None know thy naked light.
O! were the day, of Thee dim shade,
As of the soul is night,
O! who would fear when in the
    bourne's expansion,
With Thy first kiss we fade.

But the sad night shivers,
And palely wastes and dies;
A wraith under day's burning hair,
And his humid golden eyes.
He has browsed by immortal meadowed
    rivers;
O! were she nesting there!

A GIRL'S THOUGHTS

Dim apprehension of a trust
Comes over me this quiet hour,
As though the silence were a flower,
And this, its perfume, dark like dust.

My individual self would cling
Through fear, through pride, unto
    its fears.
It strives to shut out what it hears,
The founts of being, murmuring.

O! need, whose hauntings terrorize;
Whether my maiden ways would
    hide,
Or lose, and to that need subside,
Life shrinks, and instinct dreads
    surprise.

WEDDED

[I]

They leave their love-lorn haunts,
Their sigh-warm floating Eden;
And they are mute at once;
Mortals by God unheeden;
By their past kisses chidden.

But they have kist and known
Clear things we dim by guesses—
Spirit to spirit grown—
Heaven, born in hand caresses—
Love, fall from sheltering tresses.

And they are dumb and strange:
Bared trees bowed from each other.
Their last green interchange
What lost dreams shall discover?
Dead, strayed, to love-strange
        lover.

MIDSUMMER FROST *

A July ghost, aghast at the strange
    winter,
Wonders, at burning noon (all summer
    seeming),
How, like a sad thought buried in light
    words,
Winter, an alien presence, is ambushed
    here.

See, from the fire-fountained noon, there
    creep
Lazy yellow ardours towards pale
    evening,
To thread dark and vain fire
Over my unsens'd heart,
Dead heart, no urgent summer can reach.
Hidden as a root from air or a star from
    day;
A frozen pool whereon mirth dances;
Where the shining boys would fish.

My blinded brain pierced is,
And searched by a thought, and pangful
With bitter ooze of a joyous knowledge
Of some starred time outworn.
Like blind eyes that have slinked past
    God,
And light, their untasked inheritance,
(Sealed eyes that trouble never the Sun)
Yet has feel of a Maytime pierced.
He heareth the Maytime dances;
Frees from their airy prison, bright
    voices,
To loosen them in his dark imagination,

Powered with girl revels rare
And silks and merry colours,
And all the unpeopled ghosts that walk
    in words.
Till wave white hands that ripple lakes
    of sadness,
Until the sadness vanishes and the
    stagnant pool remains.

Underneath this summer air can July
    dream
How, in night hanging forest of eating
    maladies,
A frozen forest of moon unquiet mad-
    ness,
The moon-drunk haunted pierced soul
    dies;
Starved by its Babel folly, lying stark,
Unvexed by July's warm eyes.

LOVE AND LUST   *

No dream of mortal joy;
Yet all the dreamers die.
We wither with our world
To make room for her sky.

O lust! when you lie ravished,
Broken in the dust,
We will call for love in
        vain,
Finding love was lust.

IN PICCADILLY

Lamp-lit faces! to you
What is your starry dew?
Gold flowers of the night
        blue!

Deep in wet pavement's slime,
Mud rooted, is your fierce
        prime,
To bloom in lust's coloured
        clime.

The sheen of eyes that lust,
Dew, Time made your trust,
Lights your passionless dust.

A MOOD

You are so light and gay,
So slight, sweet maid;
Your limbs like leaves in play,
Or beams that grasses braid;
O! joys whose jewels pray
My breast to be inlaid.

Frail fairy of the streets;
Strong, dainty lure;
For all men's eyes the sweets
Whose lack makes hearts so poor;
While your heart loveless beats,
Light, laughing, and impure.

O! fragrant waft of flesh
Float through me so—
My limbs are in your mesh,
My blood forgets to flow.
Ah! lilied meadows fresh,
It knows where it would go.

APRIL DAWN   *

Pale light hid in light
Stirs the still day-spring;
Wavers the dull sight
With a spirit's wing.

Dreams, in frail rose mist,
Lurking to waylay,
Subtle-wise have kist
Winter into May.

Nothing to the sight . . .
Pool of pulseless air.
Spirits are in flight
And my soul their lair.

IF YOU ARE FIRE

If you are fire and I am fire,
Who blows the flame apart
So that desire eludes desire
Around one central heart?

A single root and separate bough,
And what blind hands between
That make our longing's mutual
    glow
As if it had not been?

BREAK IN BY SUBTLER WAYS *

Break in by subtler nearer ways;
Dulled closeness is too far.
And separate we are
Through joinèd days.

The shine and strange romance of
        time
In absence hides and change.
Shut eyes and hear the strange
Perfect new chime.

THE ONE LOST

I mingle with your bones.
You steal in subtle noose
This lighted dust Jehovah loans
And now I lose.

What will the Lender say
When I shall not be found,
Safe sheltered at the Judgment Day,
Being in you bound?

He'll hunt throng'd wards of
        Heaven,
Call to uncoffined earth,
'Where is this soul unjudged,
        not given
Dole for good's dearth?'

And I, lying so safe
Within you, hearing all,
To have cheated God shall laugh,
Freed by your thrall.

'MY SOUL IS ROBBED' *

[II]

My soul is robbed by your most treacherous
    eyes
Treading its intricate infinities.
Stay there, rich robbers! what I lose is dross;
Since my life is your dungeon, where is loss?

Ah! as the sun is prisoned in the heaven,
Whose walls dissolve, of their own nature
    bereaven,
So do your looks, as idly, without strife,
Cover all steeps of sense, which no more
    pasture life.
Which no more feel, but only know you
    there,
In this blind trance of some white anywhere.

Come—come—that glance engendered
    ecstasy—
That subtle unspaced mutual intimacy
Whereby two spirits of one thought
    commune
Like separate instruments that play one tune,
And the whole miracle and amazement of
The unexpected flowering of love
Concentres to an instant that expands
And takes unto itself the strangest of
    strange lands.

GOD MADE BLIND *

It were a proud God-guiling, to allure
And flatter, by some cheat of ill, our Fate
To hold back the perfect crookedness its
    hate
Devised, and keep it poor,
And ignorant of our joy—
Masked in a giant wrong of cruel annoy,
That stands as some bleak hut to frost and
    night,
While hidden in bed is warmth and mad
    delight.

For all Love's heady valour and loved pain
Towers in our sinews that may not suppress
(Shut to God's eye) Love's springing eager-
    ness,
And mind to advance his gain
Of gleeful secrecy
Through dolorous clay, which his eternity
Has pierced, in light that pushes out to meet
Eternity without us, heaven's heat.

And then, when Love's power hath in-
    creased so
That we must burst or grow to give it
    room,
And we can no more cheat our God with
    gloom,
We'll cheat Him with our joy.
For say! what can God do
To us, to Love, whom we have grown into?
Love! the poured rays of God's Eternity!
We are grown God—and shall His self-hate
    be?

* ©   41

THE DEAD HEROES

Flame out, you glorious
    skies,
Welcome our brave,
Kiss their exultant eyes;
Give what they gave.

Flash, mailèd seraphim,
Your burning spears;
New days to outflame their
    dim
Heroic years.

Thrills their baptismal tread
The bright proud air;
The embattled plumes out-
    spread
Burn upwards there.

Flame out, flame out, O
    Song!
Star ring to star,
Strong as our hurt is strong
Our children are.

Their blood is England's
    heart;
By their dead hands
It is their noble part
That England stands.

England—Time gave them
    thee;
They gave back this
To win Eternity
And claim God's kiss.

42

THE CLOISTER *

Our eyes no longer sail the tidal streets,
Nor harbour where the hours like petals
    float
By sensual treasures glittering through
    thin walls
Of woman's eyes and colour's mystery.

The roots of our eternal souls were fed
On the world's dung and now their
    blossoms gleam.
God gives to glisten in an angel's hair
These He has gardened, for they please
    His eyes.

EXPRESSION

Call—call—and bruise the air:
Shatter dumb space!
Yea!   We will fling this passion
   everywhere;
Leaving no place

For the superb and grave
Magnificent throng,
The pregnant queens of quietness
     that brave
And edge our song

Of wonder at the light
(Our life-leased home),
Of greeting to our housemates.
    And in might
Our song shall roam

Life's heart, a blossoming fire
Blown bright by thought,
While gleams and fades the infinite
    desire,
Phantasmed naught.

Can this be caught and caged?
Wings can be clipt
Of eagles, the sun's gaudy measure
    gauged,
But no sense dipt

In the mystery of sense.
The troubled throng
Of words break out like smothered
    fire through dense
And smouldering wrong.

MOSES: A PLAY

1916

SPRING 1916

Slow, rigid, is this masquerade
That passes as through granite air;
Heavily—heavily passes.
What has she fed on? Who her table laid
Through the three seasons? What forbidden
    fare
Ruined her as a mortal lass is?

I played with her two years ago,
Who might be now her own sister in stone,
So altered from her May mien,
When round pink neck a necklace of warm
    snow
Laughed to her throat where my mouth's
    touch had gone.
How is this, ruined Queen?

Who lured her vivid beauty so
To be that strained chilled thing that moves
So ghastly midst her young brood
Of pregnant shoots that she for men did
    grow?
Where are the strong men who made these
    their loves?
Spring! God pity your mood!

MOSES

PERSONS

MOSES, *an Egyptian Prince*
ABINOAH, *an overseer*
TWO HEBREWS
KOELUE, *Abinoah's Daughter*
MESSENGER

SCENE I: *Outside a college in Thebes.   Egyptian students
pass by.*   MOSES *alone in meditation.*

[*Enter* MESSENGER]

MESSENGER [*handing papyrus*] Pharaoh's desires.
MOSES [*reads*] To our beloved son, greeting.   Add to our
  thoughts of you, if possible to add, but a little, and you
  are more than old heroes.   Not to bemean your genius,
  who might cry 'Was that all!', we pile barriers every-
  where.   We give you idiots for tools, tree stumps for
  swords, skin sacks for souls.   The sixteenth pyramid
  remains to be built.   We give you the last draft of slaves.
  Move!   Forget not the edict.   PHARAOH.
MOSES [*to* MESSENGER] What is the edict?
MESSENGER. The royal paunch of Pharaoh dangled wor-
      riedly,
  Not knowing where the wrong.   Viands once giant-like
  Came to him thin and thinner.   What rats gnawed?
  Horror!   The swarm of slaves.   The satraps swore
  Their wives' bones hurt them when they lay abed
  That before were soft and plump.   The people howled
  They'd boil the slaves three days to get their fat,
  Ending the famine.   A haggard council held
  Decrees the two hind molars, those two staunchest
  Busy labourers in the belly's service, to be drawn
  From out each slave's greased mouth, which soon,

47

From incapacity, would lose the habit
Of eating.

MOSES. Well, should their bones stick out to find the air,
I'll make a use of them for pleasantness—
Droll demonstrations of anatomy.

MESSENGER. And when you've ended find 'twas one on
sharks.

[MOSES *signs to* MESSENGER *to go. Exit* MES-
SENGER]

MOSES. Fine! Fine!
See in my brain
What madmen have rushed through,
And like a tornado
Torn up the tight roots
Of some dead universe.
The old clay is broken
For a power to soak in and knit
It all into tougher tissues
To hold life,
Pricking my nerves till the brain might crack
It boils to my finger-tips,
Till my hands ache to grip
The hammer—the lone hammer
That breaks lives into a road
Through which my genius drives.
Pharaoh well peruked and oiled,
And your admirable pyramids,
And your interminable procession
Of crowded kings,
You are my little fishing rods
Wherewith I catch the fish
To suit my hungry belly.

I am rough now, and new, and will have no tailor.
Startlingly,
As a mountain-side

48

Wakes aware of its other side,
When from a cave a leopard comes,
On its heels the same red sand,
Springing with acquainted air,
Sprang an intelligence
Coloured as a whim of mine,
Showed to my dull outer eyes
The living eyes underneath.
Did I not shrivel up and take the place of air,
Secret as those eyes were,
And those strong eyes call up a giant frame?
And I am that now.

Pharaoh is sleek and deep;
And where his love for me is set—under
The deeps, on their floor, or in the shallow ways,
Though I have been as a diver—never yet
Could I find. . . . I have a way, a touchstone!
A small misdemeanour, touch of rebelliousness;
To prick the vein of father, monitor, foe,
Will tell which of these his kingship is.
If I shut my eyes to the edict,
And leave the pincers to rust,
And the slaves' teeth as God made them,
Then hide from the summoning tribunal,
Pharaoh will speak, and I'll seize that word to act.
Should the word be a foe's, I can use it well,
As a poison to soak into Egypt's bowels,
A wraith from old Nile will cry
'For his mercy they break his back'
And I shall have a great following for this,
The rude touched heart of the mauled sweaty horde,
Their rough tongues fawn at my hands, their red
    streaked eyes
Glitter with sacrifice.   Well! Pharaoh bids me act.
Hah!   I'm all a-bristle.   Lord! his eyes would go
    wide

49

If he knew the road my rampant dreams would
    race.
I am too much awake now—restless, so restless.
Behind white mists invisibly
My thoughts stood like a mountain.
But Power, watching as a man,
Saw no mountain there—
Only the mixing mist and sky,
And the flat earth.
What shoulder pushed through those mists
Of gay fantastic pastimes
And startled hills of sleep?

[*He looks in a mirror*]

Oh! apparition of me!
Ruddy flesh soon hueless!
Fade and show to my eyes
The lasting bare body.
Soul sack fall away
And show what you hold.
Sing!   Let me hear you sing.

A VOICE [*sings*]

Upon my lips, like a cloud
To burst on the peaks of light,
Sit cowled, impossible things
To tie my hands at their prime and height.
Power! break through their shroud.
Pierce them so thoroughly,
Thoroughly enter me,
Know me for one dead.
Break the shadowy thread,
The cowering spirit's bond
Writ by illusions blond.

Ah! let the morning pale
Throb with a wilder pulse.
No delicate flame shall quail

With terror at your convulse.
Thin branches whip the white skies
To lips and spaces of song
That chant a mood to my eyes. . . .
Ah! sleep can be overlong.

MOSES. Voices thunder, voices of deeds not done.
Lo! on the air are scrawled in abysmal light
Old myths never known, and yet already foregone,
And songs more lost, more secret than desert light.
Martyrdoms of uncreated things,
Virgin silences waiting a breaking voice—
As in a womb they cry, in a cage beat vain wings
Under life, over life—is their unbeing my choice?

Dull wine of torpor—the unsoldered spirit lies limp.
Ah! if she would run into a mould
Some new idea unwalled
To human by-ways, an apocalyptic camp
Of utterest and ulterior dreaming,
Understood only in its gleaming,
To flash stark naked the whole girth of the world.
I am sick of priests and forms,
This rigid dry-boned refinement.
As ladies' perfumes are
Obnoxious to stern natures,
This miasma of a rotting god
Is to me.
Who has made of the forest a park?
Who has changed the wolf to a dog?
And put the horse in harness?
And man's mind in a groove?

I heard the one spirit cry in them,
'Break this metamorphosis,
Disenchant my lying body,
Only putrefaction is free,

And I, Freedom, am not.
Moses! touch us, thou!'

There shall not be a void or calm
But a fury fill the veins of time
Whose limbs had begun to rot,
Who had flattered my stupid torpor
With an easy and mimic energy,
And drained my veins with a paltry marvel
More monstrous than battle,
For the soul ached and went out dead in pleasure.

Is not this song still sung in the streets of me?

> A naked African
> Walked in the sun
> Singing—singing
> Of his wild love.
>
> I slew the tiger
> With your young strength
> (My tawny panther)
> Rolled round my life.
>
> Three sheep, your breasts,
> And my head between,
> Grazing together
> On a smooth slope.

Ah!   Koelue!

Had you embalmed your beauty, so
It could not backward go,
Or change in any way,
What were the use, if on my eyes
The embalming spices were not laid
To keep us fixed,
Two amorous sculptures passioned endlessly?
What were the use, if my sight grew,

And its far branches were cloud-hung,
You, small at the roots, like grass?
While the new lips my spirit would kiss
Were not red lips of flesh,
But the huge kiss of power?
Where yesterday soft hair through my fingers fell
A shaggy mane would entwine,
And no slim form work fire to my thighs.
But human Life's inarticulate mass
Throb the pulse of a thing
Whose mountain flanks awry
Beg my mastery—mine!
Ah! I will ride the dizzy beast of the world
My road—my way.

SCENE II: *Evening before Thebes. The Pyramids are being
built. Swarms of Hebrews labouring. Priests and
Taskmasters. Two Hebrews are furtively talking.*
KOELUE *passes by singing.*

KOELUE.　　The vague viols of evening
　　　　　　Call all the flower clans
　　　　　　To some abysmal swinging
　　　　　　And tumult of deep trance;
　　　　　　He may hear, flower of my singing,
　　　　　　And come hither winging.
OLD HEBREW [*gazing after her in a muffled frenzy*]. Hateful
　　　　harlot.　Boils cover your small cruel face.
　　O! fine champion Moses.　O! so good to us,
　　O! grand begetter on her of a whip and a torturer,
　　Her father, born to us, since you kissed her.
　　Our champion, O! so good to us.
YOUNG HEBREW. For shame!　Our brothers' twisted
　　　　blood-smeared gums
　　Tell we only have more room for wreck curtailed,

53

For you, having no teeth to draw, it is no mercy
Perhaps, but they might mangle your gums;
Or touch a nerve somewhere.   He barred it now.
And that is all his thanks, he, too, in peril.
Be still, old man, wait a little.
OLD HEBREW.   Wait!
All day some slow dark quadruped beats
To pulp our springiness.
All day some hoofed animal treads our veins,
Leisurely—leisurely our energies flow out.
All agonies created from the first day
Have wandered hungry searching the world for us,
Or they would perish like disused Behemoth.
Is our Messiah one to unleash these agonies
As Moses does, who gives us an Abinoah?
YOUNG HEBREW. Yesterday as I lay nigh dead with toil
Underneath the hurtling crane oiled with our blood,
Thinking to end all and let the crane crush me,
He came by and bore me into the shade.
O what a furnace roaring in his blood
Thawed my congealed sinews and tingled my own
Raging through me like a strong cordial.
He spoke! since yesterday
Am I not larger grown?
I've seen men hugely shapen in soul
Of such unhuman shaggy male turbulence
They tower in foam miles from our neck-strained
     sight.
And to their shop only heroes come.
But all were cripples to this speed
Constrained to the stables of flesh.
I say there is a famine in ripe harvest
When hungry giants come as guests.
Come knead the hills and ocean into food.
There is none for him.
The streaming vigours of his blood erupting
From his halt tongue are like an anger thrust

54

Out of a madman's piteous craving for
A monstrous balked perfection.

OLD HEBREW. He is a prince, an animal
  Not of our kind, who perhaps has heard
  Vague rumours of our world, to his mind
  An unpleasant miasma.

YOUNG HEBREW. Is not Miriam his sister, Jochabed his
      mother?
  In the womb he looked round and saw
  From furthermost stretches our wrong.
  From the palaces and schools
  Our pain has pierced dead generations
  Back to his blood's thin source.
  As we lie chained by Egyptian men
  He lay in nets of their women,
  And now rejoice, he has broken their meshes.
  O! his desires are fleets of treasure
  He has squandered in treacherous seas
  Sailing mistrust to find frank ports.
  He fears our fear and tampers mildly
  For our assent to let him save us.
  When he walks amid our toil
  With some master-mason
  His tense brows critical
  Of the loose enginery—
  Hints famed devices flat, his rod
  Scratching new schemes on the sand.
  But read hard the scrawled lines there—
  Limned turrets and darkness, chinks of light,
  Half beasts snorting into the light,
  A phantasmagoria, wild escapade
  To our hearts' clue; just a daring plan
  To the honest mason.   What swathed meanings
      peer
  From his workaday council, washed to and from
  Your understanding till you doubt
  That a word was said.

But a terror wakes and forces your eyes
Into his covertly, to search his searching.
Startled to life starved hopes slink out
Cowering, incredulous.

OLD HEBREW [*to himself*]. His youth is flattered at Moses'
kind speech to him.

[*To the* YOUNG HEBREW]

I am broken and grey, have seen much in my time,
And all this gay grotesque of childish man
Long passed. Half blind, half deaf, I only grumble
I am not blind or deaf enough for peace.
I have seen splendid young fools cheat themselves
Into a prophet's frenzy; I have seen
So many crazed shadows puffed away,
And conscious cheats with such an ache for fame
They'd make a bonfire of themselves to be
Mouthed in the squares, broad in the public eye.
And whose backs break, whose lives are mauled, after
It all falls flat?   His tender airs chill me
As thoughts of sleep to a man tiptoed night-long
Roped round his neck, for sleep means death to him.
Oh! he is kind to us.
Your safe teeth chatter when they hear a step.
He left them yours because his cunning way
Would brag the wrong against his humane act
By Pharaoh; so gain more favour than he lost.

YOUNG HEBREW. Help him not then, and push your
safety away.
I for my part will be his backward eye,
His hands when they are shut.   Ah! Abinoah!
Like a bad smell from the soul of Moses dipt
In the mire of lust, he hangs round him.
And if his slit-like eyes could tear right out
The pleasure Moses on his daughter had,
She'd be as virgin as ere she came nestling
Into that fierce unmanageable blood,

56

Flying from her loathed father.   O, that slave
Has hammered from the anvil of her beauty
A steel to break his manacles.   Hard for us,
Moses has made him overseer.   O, his slits
Pry—pry . . . for what? . . . to sell to Imra. . . .

[ABINOAH *is seen approaching*]

Sh! the thin-lipped abomination!
Zigzagging haschish tours in a fine style.
It were delightful labour making bricks,
Knowing they would kiss friendly with his head.

ABINOAH [*who has been taking haschish, and has one ob-
       session, hatred of Jews*]. Dirt-draggled mongrels,
       circumcised slaves.
You puddle with your lousy gibberish
The holy air, Pharaoh's own tributary.
Filthy manure for Pharaoh's flourishing.
I'll circumcise and make holy your tongues,
And stop one outlet to your profanation.

[*To the* OLD HEBREW]

I've never seen one beg so for a blow,
Too soft am I to resist such entreaty.

[*Beats him*]

Your howling holds the earnest energies
You cheat from Pharaoh when you make his bricks.

AN AGED MINSTREL [*sings from a distance*]

Taut is the air and tied the trees,
The leaves lie as on a hand.
God's unthinkable imagination
Invents new tortures for nature.

And when the air is soft and the leaves
Feel free and push and tremble,
Will they not remember and say
How wonderful to have lived?

[*The* OLD HEBREW *is agitated and murmurs*]

Messiah, Messiah . . . that voice . . .

O, he has beaten my sight out. . . . I see
Like a rain about a devouring fire. . . .

[*The Minstrel sings*]

Ye who best God awhile,—O, hear, your wealth
Is but His cunning to see to make death more hard.
Your iron sinews take more pain in breaking.
And he has made the market for your beauty
Too poor to buy although you die to sell.

OLD HEBREW. I am crazed with whips. . . . I hear a
Messiah.

YOUNG HEBREW. The venerable man will question this.

ABINOAH [*overhearing*]. I'll beat you more, and he'll question
The scratchiness of your whining; or may be,
Thence may be born deep argument
With reasons from philosophy
That this blow, taking longer, yet was but one,
Or perhaps two; or that you felt this one—
Arguing from the difference in your whine—
Exactly, or not, like the other.

MINSTREL. You labour hard to give pain.

ABINOAH [*still beating*]. My pain is . . . not . . . to labour so.

MINSTREL. What is this greybeard worth to you now,
All his dried-up blood crumbled to dust?

[*Motions* ABINOAH *to desist, but not in time to
prevent the old man fainting into the hands of
the* YOUNG HEBREW]

ABINOAH. Harper, are you envious of the old fool?
Go! hug the rat who stole your last crumbs,
And gnawed the hole in your life which made Time
wonder
Who it was saved labour for him the next score of
years.
We allowed them life for their labour—they haggled.
Food they must have—and (god of laughter!) even
ease;

58

But mud and lice and Jews are very busy
Breeding plagues in ease.

[*The Minstrel pulls his beard and robe off*]

ABINOAH. Moses!
MOSES. You drunken rascal!
ABINOAH. A drunken rascal! Isis! hear the Prince.
  Drunken with duty, and he calls me rascal.
MOSES. You may think it your duty to get drunk;
  But get yourself bronze claws before
  You would be impudent.
ABINOAH. When a man's drunk he'll kiss a horse or king,
  He's so affectionate. Under your words
  There is strong wine to make me drunk; you think,
  The lines of all your face say, 'Her father, Koelue's
    father.'
MOSES. This is too droll and extraordinary.
  I dreamt I was a prince, a queer droll dream,
  Where a certain slave of mine, a thing, a toad,
  Shifting his belly, showed a diamond
  Where he had lain. And a blind dumb messenger
  Bore syllabled messages soaked right through with
    glee.
  I paid the toad—the blind man; afterwards
  They spread a stench and snarling. O, droll dream!
  I think you merely mean to flatter me,
  You subtle knave, that, more than prince, I'm *man*,
  And worth to listen to your bawdy breath.
ABINOAH. Yet my breath was worth your mixing with.
MOSES. A boy at college flattered so by a girl
  Will give her what she asks for.
ABINOAH. Osiris! burning Osiris!
  Of thee desirable, for thee, her hair. . . .

[*He looks inanely at* MOSES, *saying to himself*]

Prince Imra vowed his honey-hives and vineyards.
Isis! to let a Jew have her for nothing.

[*He sings under his breath*]
Night by night in a little house
A man and woman meet.
They look like each other,
They are sister and brother;
And night by night at that
          same hour
A king calls for his son in vain.

MOSES [*to himself*]. So, sister Miriam, it is known then.
          Slave, you die.
     [*Aloud*] O, you ambiguous stench.
     You'll be more interesting as a mummy
     I have no doubt.

ABINOAH. I'm drunk, yes—drenched with the thought
     Of a certain thing.   [*Aside*] I'll sleep sounder to-night
     Than all the nights I've followed him about,
     Worrying each slight clue, each monosyllable
     To give the word to Imra.   The prince is near,
     And Moses' eyes shall blink before next hour
     To a hundred javelins.   I'll tease him till they come
     [*Aloud*] On Koelue's tears I swam to you, in a mist
     Of her sighs I hung round you,
     As in some hallucination I've been walking
     A white waste world, we two only in it.

MOSES. Doubtless the instinct balked to bully the girl,
     Making large gapings in your haschish dreams,
     Led you to me, in whom she was thoroughly lost.
     Pah! you sicken me.

          [*He is silent awhile, then turns away*]

ABINOAH. Prince Imra is Pharaoh's choice now, and
          Koelue's.

          [MOSES *turns back menacingly*]

MOSES. Silence, you beast!

          [*He changes his tone to a winning softness*]

     I hate these family quarrels: it is so

Like fratricide.   I am a rebel, well?
Soft!   You are not, and we are knit so close
It would be shame for a son to be so honoured
And the father still unknown.   Come, Koelue's (so
    my) father,
I'll tell my plans.   You'll beg to be rebel, then.
Look round on the night,
Old as the first, bleak, even her wish is done;
She has never seen, though dreamt perhaps of the
    sun,
Yet only dawn divides; could a miracle
Destroy the dawn, night would be mixed with light,
No night or light would be, but a new thing.
So with these slaves, who perhaps have dreamt of
    freedom,
Egypt was in the way; I'll strike it out
With my ways curious and unusual.
I have a trouble in my mind for largeness,
Rough-hearted, shaggy, which your grave ardours
    lack.
Here is the quarry quiet for me to hew,
Here are the springs, primeval elements,
The roots' hid secrecy, old source of race,
Unreasoned reason of the savage instinct.
I'd shape one impulse through the contraries
Of vain ambitious men, selfish and callous,
And frail life-drifters, reticent, delicate.
Litheness thread bulk; a nation's harmony.
These are not lame, nor bent awry, but placeless
With the rust and stagnant.   All that's low I'll charm;
Barbaric love sweeten to tenderness.
Cunning run into wisdom, craft turn to skill.
Their meanness threaded right and sensibly
Change to a prudence, envied and not sneered.
Their hugeness be a driving wedge to a thing,
Ineffable and useable, as near
Solidity as human life can be.

61

So grandly fashion these rude elements
Into some newer nature, a consciousness
Like naked light seizing the all-eyed soul,
Oppressing with its gorgeous tyranny
Until they take it thus—or die.

> [*While speaking, he places his hand on the unsuspecting Egyptian's head and gently pulls his hair back (caressingly), until his chin is above his forehead, and holds him so till he is suffocated. In the darkness ahead is seen the glimmer of javelins and spears. It is Prince Imra's cohorts come to arrest* MOSES]

GOD

In his malodorous brain what slugs and mire,
Lanthorned in his oblique eyes, guttering burned!
His body lodged a rat where men nursed souls.
The world flashed grape-green eyes of a foiled cat
To him.   On fragments of an old shrunk power,
On shy and maimed, on women wrung awry,
He lay, a bullying hulk, to crush them more.
But when one, fearless, turned and clawed like
  bronze,
Cringing was easy to blunt these stern paws,
And he would weigh the heavier on those after.

Who rests in God's mean flattery now?   Your
  wealth
Is but his cunning to make death more hard.
Your iron sinews take more pain in breaking.
And he has made the market for your beauty
Too poor to buy, although you die to sell.
Only that he has never heard of sleep;
And when the cats come out the rats are sly.
Here we are safe till he slinks in at dawn.

But he has gnawed a fibre from strange roots,
And in the morning some pale wonder ceases.
Things are not strange and strange things are
  forgetful.
Ah! if the day were arid, somehow lost
Out of us, but it is as hair of us,
And only in the hush no wind stirs it.
And in the light vague trouble lifts and breathes,
And restlessness still shadows the lost ways.
The fingers shut on voices that pass through,
Where blind farewells are taken easily. . . .

Ah! this miasma of a rotting God!

FIRST FRUIT

I did not pluck at all,
And I am sorry now,
The garden is not barred,
But the boughs are heavy with snow,
The flake-blossoms thickly fall,
And the hid roots sigh, 'How long will
    our flowers be marred?'

Strange as a bird were dumb,
Strange as a hueless leaf.
As one deaf hungers to hear,
Or gazes without belief,
The fruit yearned 'Fingers, come'.
O, shut hands, be empty another year.

CHAGRIN

Caught still as Absalom,
Surely the air hangs
From the swayless cloud-boughs,
Like hair of Absalom
Caught and hanging still.

From the imagined weight
Of spaces in a sky
Of mute chagrin, my thoughts
Hang like branch-clung hair
To trunks of silence swung,
With the choked soul weighing down
Into thick emptiness.
Christ! end this hanging death,
For endlessness hangs therefrom.

Invisibly—branches break
From invisible trees—
The cloud-woods where we rush,
Our eyes holding so much,
Which we must ride dim ages round
Ere the hands (we dream) can touch,
We ride, we ride, before the morning
The secret roots of the sun to tread,
And suddenly
We are lifted of all we know
And hang from implacable boughs.

MARCHING

(AS SEEN FROM THE LEFT FILE)

My eyes catch ruddy necks
Sturdily pressed back—
All a red brick moving glint.
Like flaming pendulums, hands
Swing across the khaki—
Mustard-coloured khaki—
To the automatic feet.

We husband the ancient glory
In these bared necks and hands.
Not broke is the forge of Mars;
But a subtler brain beats iron
To shoe the hoofs of death
(Who paws dynamic air now).
Blind fingers loose an iron cloud
To rain immortal darkness
On strong eyes.

SLEEP

Godhead's lip hangs
When our pulses have no golden tremors,
And his whips are flicked by mice
And all star-amorous things.

Drops, drops of shivering quiet
Filter under my lids.
Now only am I powerful.
What though the cunning gods outwit us
    here
In daytime and in playtime,
Surely they feel the gyves we lay on them
In our sleep.

O, subtle gods lying hidden!
O, gods with your oblique eyes!
Your elbows in the dawn, and wrists
Bright with the afternoon,
Do you not shake when a mortal slides
Into your own unvexed peace?
When a moving stillness breaks over your
    knees
(An emanation of piled æons' pressure)
From our bodies flat and straight,
And your limbs are locked,
Futilely gods',
And shut your sinister essences?

HEART'S FIRST WORD

[II]

And all her soft dark hair,
Breathed for him like a prayer.
And her white lost face,
Was prisoned to some far place.
Love was not denied—
Love's ends would hide.
And flower and fruit and tree
Were under its sea.
Yea! its abundance knelt
Where the nerves felt
The springs of feeling flow
And made pain grow.
There seemed no root or sky
But a pent infinity
Where apparitions dim
Sculptured each whim
In flame and wandering mist
Of kisses to be kist.

TRENCH POEMS
1916–1918

THE TROOP SHIP

Grotesque and queerly huddled
Contortionists to twist
The sleepy soul to a sleep,
We lie all sorts of ways
And cannot sleep.
The wet wind is so cold,
And the lurching men so careless,
That, should you drop to a doze,
Winds' fumble or men's feet
Are on your face.

AUGUST 1914   *

What in our lives is burnt
In the fire of this?
The heart's dear granary?
The much we shall miss?

Three lives hath one life—
Iron, honey, gold.
The gold, the honey gone—
Left is the hard and cold.

Iron are our lives
Molten right through our youth.
A burnt space through ripe fields
A fair mouth's broken tooth.

THE JEW

Moses, from whose loins I sprung,
Lit by a lamp in his blood
Ten immutable rules, a moon
For mutable lampless men.

The blonde, the bronze, the ruddy,
With the same heaving blood,
Keep tide to the moon of Moses.
Then why do they sneer at me?

LUSITANIA   *

Chaos! that coincides with this militant
    purpose.
Chaos! the heart of this earnest malignancy.
Chaos! that helps, chaos that gives to shatter
Mind-wrought, mind-unimagining energies
For topless ill, of dynamite and iron.
Soulless logic, inventive enginery.
Now you have got the peace-faring *Lusitania*,
Germany's gift—all earth they would give thee,
    Chaos.

FROM FRANCE *

The spirit drank the café lights;
All the hot life that glittered there,
And heard men say to women gay,
'Life is just so in France'.

The spirit dreams of café lights,
And golden faces and soft tones,
And hears men groan to broken men,
'This is not Life in France'.

Heaped stones and a charred signboard
    show
With grass between and dead folk under,
And some birds sing, while the spirit takes
    wing.
And this is Life in France.

BREAK OF DAY IN THE TRENCHES

The darkness crumbles away—
It is the same old druid Time as ever.
Only a live thing leaps my hand—
A queer sardonic rat—
As I pull the parapet's poppy
To stick behind my ear.
Droll rat, they would shoot you if they
    knew
Your cosmopolitan sympathies.
Now you have touched this English hand
You will do the same to a German—
Soon, no doubt, if it be your pleasure
To cross the sleeping green between.
It seems you inwardly grin as you pass
Strong eyes, fine limbs, haughty athletes
Less chanced than you for life,
Bonds to the whims of murder,
Sprawled in the bowels of the earth,
The torn fields of France.
What do you see in our eyes
At the shrieking iron and flame
Hurled through still heavens?
What quaver—what heart aghast?
Poppies whose roots are in man's veins
Drop, and are ever dropping;
But mine in my ear is safe,
Just a little white with the dust.

'A WORM FED ON THE HEART OF CORINTH' *

A worm fed on the heart of
    Corinth,
Babylon and Rome:
Not Paris raped tall Helen,
But this incestuous worm,
Who lured her vivid beauty
To his amorphous sleep.
England! famous as Helen
Is thy betrothal sung
To him the shadowless,
More amorous than Solomon.

HOME-THOUGHTS FROM FRANCE

Wan, fragile faces of joy!
Pitiful mouths that strive
To light with smiles the place
We dream we walk alive.

To you I stretch my hands,
Hands shut in pitiless trance
In a land of ruin and woe,
The desolate land of France.

Dear faces startled and shaken,
Out of wild dust and sounds
You yearn to me, lure and sadden
My heart with futile bounds.

THE DYING SOLDIER

'Here are houses', he moaned,
'I could reach but my brain swims.'
Then they thundered and flashed
And shook the earth to its rims.

'They are gunpits', he gasped,
'Our men are at the guns.
Water—water—O water
For one of England's dying sons.'

'We cannot give you water
Were all England in your breath.'
'Water—water—O water'
He moaned and swooned to death.

IN WAR

Fret the nonchalant noon
With your spleen
Or your gay brow,
For the motion of your spirit
Ever moves with these.

When day shall be too quiet,
Deaf to you
And your dumb smile,
Untuned air shall lap the stillness
In the old space for your voice—

The voice that once could mirror
Remote depths
Of moving being,
Stirred by responsive voices near,
Suddenly stilled for ever.

No ghost darkens the places
Dark to One;
But my eyes dream,
And my heart is heavy to think
How it was heavy once.

In the old days when death
Stalked the world
For the flower of men,
And the rose of beauty faded
And pined in the great gloom,

One day we dug a grave:
We were vexed
With the sun's heat.
We scanned the hooded dead:
At noon we sat and talked.

How death had kissed their eyes
Three dread noons since,
How human art won
The dark soul to flicker
Till it was lost again:

And we whom chance kept whole—
But haggard,
Spent—were charged
To make a place for them who knew
No pain in any place.

The good priest came to pray;
Our ears half heard,
And half we thought
Of alien things, irrelevant;
And the heat and thirst were great.

The good priest read: 'I heard . . .
Dimly my brain
Held words and lost. . . .
Sudden my blood ran cold. . . .
God! God! it could not be.

He read my brother's name;
I sank—
I clutched the priest.
They did not tell me it was he
Was killed three days ago.

What are the great sceptred dooms
To us, caught
In the wild wave?
We break ourselves on them,
My brother, our hearts and years.

THE IMMORTALS

I killed them, but they would not die.
Yea! all the day and all the night
For them I could not rest nor sleep,
Nor guard from them nor hide in flight

Then in my agony I turned
And made my hands red in their gore.
In vain—for faster than I slew
They rose more cruel than before.

I killed and killed with slaughter mad;
I killed till all my strength was gone.
And still they rose to torture me,
For Devils only die for fun.

I used to think the Devil hid
In women's smiles and wine's carouse.
I called him Satan, Balzebub.
But now I call him dirty louse.

LOUSE HUNTING

Nudes—stark and glistening,
Yelling in lurid glee.   Grinning faces
And raging limbs
Whirl over the floor one fire.
For a shirt verminously busy
Yon soldier tore from his throat, with oaths
Godhead might shrink at, but not the lice.
And soon the shirt was aflare
Over the candle he'd lit while we lay.

Then we all sprang up and stript
To hunt the verminous brood.
Soon like a demons' pantomime
The place was raging.
See the silhouettes agape,
See the gibbering shadows
Mixed with the battled arms on the wall.
See gargantuan hooked fingers
Pluck in supreme flesh
To smutch supreme littleness.
See the merry limbs in hot Highland fling
Because some wizard vermin
Charmed from the quiet this revel
When our ears were half lulled
By the dark music
Blown from Sleep's trumpet.

RETURNING, WE HEAR THE LARKS

Sombre the night is.
And though we have our lives, we know
What sinister threat lurks there.

Dragging these anguished limbs, we only
    know
This poison-blasted track opens on our
    camp—
On a little safe sleep.

But hark! joy—joy—strange joy.
Lo! heights of night ringing with unseen
    larks.
Music showering on our upturned list'ning
    faces.

Death could drop from the dark
As easily as song—
But song only dropped,
Like a blind man's dreams on the sand
By dangerous tides,
Like a girl's dark hair for she dreams no
    ruin lies there,
Or her kisses where a serpent hides.

DEAD MAN'S DUMP

The plunging limbers over the shattered
    track
Racketed with their rusty freight,
Stuck out like many crowns of thorns,
And the rusty stakes like sceptres old
To stay the flood of brutish men
Upon our brothers dear.

The wheels lurched over sprawled dead
But pained them not, though their bones
    crunched,
Their shut mouths made no moan.
They lie there huddled, friend and foeman,
Man born of man, and born of woman,
And shells go crying over them
From night till night and now.

Earth has waited for them,
All the time of their growth
Fretting for their decay:
Now she has them at last!
In the strength of their strength
Suspended—stopped and held.

What fierce imaginings their dark souls lit?
Earth! have they gone into you!
Somewhere they must have gone,
And flung on your hard back
Is their soul's sack
Emptied of God-ancestralled essences.
Who hurled them out?   Who hurled?

None saw their spirits' shadow shake the
    grass,
Or stood aside for the half used life to pass

81

Out of those doomed nostrils and the
    doomed mouth,
When the swift iron burning bee
Drained the wild honey of their youth.

What of us who, flung on the shrieking
    pyre,
Walk, our usual thoughts untouched,
Our lucky limbs as on ichor fed,
Immortal seeming ever?
Perhaps when the flames beat loud on us,
A fear may choke in our veins
And the startled blood may stop.

The air is loud with death,
The dark air spurts with fire,
The explosions ceaseless are.
Timelessly now, some minutes past,
These dead strode time with vigorous life,
Till the shrapnel called 'An end!'
But not to all.   In bleeding pangs
Some borne on stretchers dreamed of home,
Dear things, war-blotted from their hearts.

Maniac Earth! howling and flying, your
    bowel
Seared by the jagged fire, the iron love,
The impetuous storm of savage love.
Dark Earth! dark Heavens! swinging in
    chemic smoke,
What dead are born when you kiss each
    soundless soul
With lightning and thunder from your
    mined heart,
Which man's self dug, and his blind fingers
    loosed?

A man's brains splattered on
A stretcher-bearer's face;
His shook shoulders slipped their load,
But when they bent to look again
The drowning soul was sunk too deep
For human tenderness.

They left this dead with the older dead,
Stretched at the cross roads.

Burnt black by strange decay
Their sinister faces lie,
The lid over each eye,
The grass and coloured clay
More motion have than they,
Joined to the great sunk silences.

Here is one not long dead;
His dark hearing caught our far wheels,
And the choked soul stretched weak hands
To reach the living word the far wheels said,
The blood-dazed intelligence beating for
      light,
Crying through the suspense of the far tor-
      turing wheels
Swift for the end to break
Or the wheels to break,
Cried as the tide of the world broke over
      his sight.

Will they come?   Will they ever come?
Even as the mixed hoofs of the mules,
The quivering-bellied mules,
And the rushing wheels all mixed
With his tortured upturned sight.
So we crashed round the bend,

We heard his weak scream,
We heard his very last sound,
And our wheels grazed his dead face.

DAUGHTERS OF WAR

Space beats the ruddy freedom of their limbs—
Their naked dances with man's spirit naked
By the root side of the tree of life
(The under side of things
And shut from earth's profoundest eyes).

I saw in prophetic gleams
These mighty daughters in their dances
Beckon each soul aghast from its crimson corpse
To mix in their glittering dances.
I heard the mighty daughters' giant sighs
In sleepless passion for the sons of valour,
And envy of the days of flesh
Barring their love with mortal boughs across—
The mortal boughs, the mortal tree of life.
The old bark burnt with iron wars
They blow to a live flame
To char the young green days
And reach the occult soul; they have no softer
        lure—
No softer lure than the savage ways of death.
We were satisfied of our lords the moon and
        the sun
To take our wage of sleep and bread and
        warmth—
These maidens came—these strong everliving
        Amazons,
And in an easy might their wrists
Of night's sway and noon's sway the sceptres
        brake,
Clouding the wild—the soft lustres of our eyes.

Clouding the wild lustres, the clinging tender
        lights;
Driving the darkness into the flame of day

With the Amazonian wind of them
Over our corroding faces
That must be broken—broken for evermore
So the soul can leap out
Into their huge embraces.
Though there are human faces
Best sculptures of Deity,
And sinews lusted after
By the Archangels tall,
Even these must leap to the love-heat of these
    maidens
From the flame of terrene days,
Leaving grey ashes to the wind—to the wind.

One (whose great lifted face,
Where wisdom's strength and beauty's strength
And the thewed strength of large beasts
Moved and merged, gloomed and lit)
Was speaking, surely, as the earth-men's earth
    fell away;
Whose new hearing drank the sound
Where pictures lutes and mountains mixed
With the loosed spirit of a thought.
Essenced to language, thus—

'My sisters force their males
From the doomed earth, from the doomed glee
And hankering of hearts.
Frail hands gleam up through the human quag-
    mire and lips of ash
Seem to wail, as in sad faded paintings
Far sunken and strange.
My sisters have their males
Clean of the dust of old days
That clings about those white hands
And yearns in those voices sad.

But these shall not see them,
Or think of them in any days or years;
They are my sisters' lovers in other days and
    years.'

SOLDIER: TWENTIETH CENTURY

I love you, great new Titan!
Am I not you?
Napoleon and Caesar
Out of you grew.

Out of unthinkable torture,
Eyes kissed by death,
Won back to the world again,
Lost and won in a breath,

Cruel men are made immortal,
Out of your pain born.
They have stolen the sun's power
With their feet on your shoulders
    worn.

Let them shrink from your girth,
That has outgrown the pallid days,
When you slept like Circe's swine,
Or a word in the brain's ways.

GIRL TO SOLDIER ON LEAVE

I love you—Titan lover,
My own storm-days' Titan.
Greater than the son of Zeus,
I know whom I would choose.

Titan—my splendid rebel—
The old Prometheus
Wanes like a ghost before your
          power—
His pangs were joys to yours.

Pallid days arid and wan
Tied your soul fast.
Babel-cities' smoky tops
Pressed upon your growth

Weary gyves.   What were you
But a word in the brain's ways,
Or the sleep of Circe's swine?
One gyve holds you yet.

It held you hiddenly on the Somme
Tied from my heart at home.
O must it loosen now?   I wish
You were bound with the old old
          gyves.

Love! you love me—your eyes
Have looked through death at mine.
You have tempted a grave too much.
I let you—I repine.

THE BURNING OF THE TEMPLE

Fierce wrath of Solomon
Where sleepest thou?   O see
The fabric which thou won
Earth and ocean to give thee—
O look at the red skies.

Or hath the sun plunged down?
What is this molten gold—
These thundering fires blown
Through heaven—where the smoke
    rolled?
Again the great king dies.

His dreams go out in smoke,
His days he let not pass
And sculptured here are broke,
Are charred as the burnt grass,
Gone as his mouth's last sighs.

THE DESTRUCTION OF JERUSALEM
BY THE BABYLONIAN HORDES

They left their Babylon bare
Of all its tall men,
Of all its proud horses;
They made for Lebanon.

And shadowy sowers went
Before their spears to sow
The fruit whose taste is ash
For Judah's soul to know.

They who bowed to the Bull god
Whose wings roofed Babylon,
In endless hosts darkened
The bright-heavened Lebanon.

They washed their grime in pools
Where laughing girls forgot
The wiles they used for Solomon.
Sweet laughter! remembered not.

Sweet laughter charred in the flame
That clutched the cloud and earth
While Solomon's towers crashed
  between,
The gird of Babylon's mirth.

'THROUGH THESE PALE COLD DAYS' *

Through these pale cold days
What dark faces burn
Out of three thousand years,
And their wild eyes yearn,

While underneath their brows
Like waifs their spirits grope
For the pools of Hebron again—
For Lebanon's summer slope.

They leave these blond still
 days
In dust behind their tread
They see with living eyes
How long they have been dead.

THE UNICORN

[*For nearly a year before his death Rosenberg had been working intermittently, as opportunity offered, on a play called 'The Unicorn'. It was never finished, and the sections and fragments of it that exist (some of them undecipherable in places) belong to several different conceptions of the play. First came 'The Amulet' which Rosenberg finished and sent home for typing.*]

THE AMULET

LILITH. SAUL. AMAK. NUBIAN

LILITH *sits under pomegranate trees watching* AMAK *playing with his father's helm and spear. A light smoke is ascending from the chimney of the hut, and through the doorway a naked Nubian man is seen stirring the embers.* SAUL *sleeps.*

LILITH. Amak, you'll break your father's sleep,
Come here and tell me what those spices are
This strange man bakes our cakes with.
It makes the brain wild.   Be still, Amak.
I'll give you the strange man your father brought
And he will run with you upon his back to-day.
Come from your father or you'll get no cake;
He's been a long journey.
Bring me the pictured book he brought for you.
What!   Already cut to pieces?
Put away that horn from your father's ear
And stay that horrid noise: come, Amak.

        [AMAK *runs to his mother with a jade amulet,
        shouting*]

AMAK. Look, mother, what I've found.

        [*He runs back again, making great shouts*]

LILITH. It dances with my blood.   When my eyes caught
    it first
I was like lost and yearned, and yearned and yearned,
And strained like iron to stay my head from falling
Upon that beggar's breast where the jade stone hung.
Perhaps the spirit of Saul's young love lies here
Strayed far and brought back by this stranger near.
Saul said his discourse was more deep than Heaven.
For the storm trapped him ere he left the town
Loaded with our week's victuals.   The slime clung
And licked and clawed and chewed the clogged
    dragging wheels

94

Till they sunk right to the axle.   Saul sodden and
    vexed
Like fury smote the mules' mouths, pulling but sweat
From his drowned hair and theirs, while the thunder
    knocked
And all the air yawned water, falling water,
And the light cart was water, like a wrecked raft,
And all seemed like a forest under the ocean.
Sudden the lightning flashed upon a figure
Moving as a man moves in the slipping mud
But singing not as a man sings, through the storm,
Which could not drown his sounds.   Saul bawled 'Hi!
    Hi!'
And the man loomed, naked vast, and gripped the
    wheels.
Saul fiercely dug from under.   He tugged the wheels,
The mules foamed, straining, straining,
Sudden they went.
Saul and the man leaped in, Saul miserably sodden
Marvelled at the large cheer in a naked glistening
    man,
And soon fell in with that contented mood,
That when our hut's light broke on his new mind
He could not credit it.   Too soon it seemed.
The strange man's talk was witchery.
I pray his baking be as magical.
The cakes should be nigh burnt.

[*She calls the* NUBIAN.   *He answers from within*]

NUBIAN. They are laid by to cool, housewife.
LILITH. Bring me the sherbet from the ledge and the fast-
    dried figs.

[*The* NUBIAN *brings sherbet and figs and a bowl of
    ice and lays them down*]
[*She looks curiously at him.   He is an immense
    man with squat, mule-skinned features: his jet-
    black curled beard, crisp hair, glistening nude*]

*limbs, appear to her like some heathen idol of
ancient stories*]
[*She thinks to herself*]

Out of the lightning
In a dizzying cloven wink
This apparition stood up,
Of stricken trunk or beast spirit,
Stirred by Saul's blasphemies.
So Saul's heart feared aghast.
But lo, he touched the mischance and life ran straight.
Was it the storm-spirit, storm's pilot
With all the heaving débris of Noah's sunken days
Dragged on his loins,
Law's spirit wandering to us
Through Nature's anarchy,
Wandering towards us when the Titans yet were
        young?
Perhaps Moses and Buddha he met.

[*She speaks aloud*]

The shadow of these pomegranate boughs
Is sweet and restful.   Sit and ease your feet.   Eat of
        these figs,
You have journeyed long.

NUBIAN. All my life, housewife.

LILITH. You have seen men and women,
    Soaked yourself in powers and old glories,
    In broken days and tears and glees,
    And touched cold hands—
    Hands shut in pitiless trances where the feast is high.
    I think there is more sorrow in the world
    Than man can bear.

NUBIAN. None can exceed their limit, lady:
    You either bear or break.

LILITH. Can one choose to break?   To bear,
    To wearily bear, is misery.
    Beauty is this corroding malady.

96

NUBIAN. Beauty is a great paradox—
Music's secret soul creeping about the senses
To wrestle with man's coarser nature.
It is hard when beauty loses.
LILITH. I think beauty is a bad bargain made of life.
Men's iron sinews hew them room in the world
And use deceits to gain them trophies.
O, when our beauty fails us did we not use
Deceits, where were our room in the world—
Only our room in the world?
Are not the songs and devices of men
Moulds they have made after my scarlet mouth,
Of cunning words and haughty contours of bronze
And viols and gathered air?
They without song have sung me
Boldly and shamelessly.
I am no wanton, no harlot;
I have been pleased and smiled my pleasure,
I am a wife with a woman's natural ways.
Yet through the shadow of the pomegranates
Filters a poison day by day,
And to a malady turns
The blond, the ample music of my heart.
Inward to eat my heart
My thoughts are worms that suck my softness all away.
I watch the dumb eyeless hours
Drop their tears, then shapeless moaning drop.
Unfathomable is my mouth's dream
Do not men say?
So secret are my far eyes,
Weaving for iron men profound subtleties.

Sorceress they name me;
And my eyes harden, and they say,
'How may those eyes know love
If God made her without a heart?

'Her tears, her moaning,
Her sad profound gaze,
The dishevelled lustres of her hair
Moon-storm like', they say,
'These are her subtleties', men say.
My husband sleeps,
The ghosts of my virgin days do not trouble him.
His sleep can be over-long,
For there is that in my embers
Pride and blushes of fire, the outraged blood,
His sleep makes me remember.

Sleep! hairy hunter, sleep!
You are not hungry more
Having fed on my deliciousness.
Your sleep is not adultery to me,
For you were wed to a girl
And I am a woman.
My lonely days are not whips to my honour.
       [*She dries her tears with her hair, then fingers the
          amulet at her throat*]
Yours, friend.
NUBIAN [*eagerly*] My amulet!   My amulet!
  [*He speaks gravely*]   Small comfort is counsel to broken
      lives,
But tolerance is medicinal.
In all our textures are loosed
Pulses straining against strictness
Because an easy issue lies therefrom.
(Could they but slink past the hands holding whips
To hunt them from the human pale
Where is the accident to cover?   Spite fears bias.)
I am justified at my heart's plea.
He is justified also.

For the eyes of vanity are sleepless—are suspicious.
Are mad with imaginings

Of secret stabs in words, in looks, in gestures.
Man is a chimera's eremite,
That lures him from the good kindness of days
Which only asks his willingness.

There is a crazed shadow from no golden body
That poisons at the core
What smiles may stray.
It mixes with all God-ancestralled essences
And twists the brain and heart.
This shadow sits in the texture of Saul's being,
Mauling your love and beauty with its lies:
I hold a power like light to shrivel it.
There, in your throat's hollow—that green jade.

> [*He snatches at it as she lets it fall. He grows
> white and troubled, and walks to where* AMAK
> *is playing, and sees minutely strewn pieces of
> paper*]

[*He mutters*] Lost—lost.
The child has torn the scroll in it
And half is away.   It cannot be spelt now.

LILITH. God, restore me his love.
  Ah!   Well!

> [*She rises*]

I will go now prepare our evening meal
And waken my husband, my lover once.

NUBIAN [*musing*]   The lightning of the heavens
  Lifts an apocalypse.
  The dumb night's lips are seared and wide,
  The world is reeling with sound.
  Was I deaf before, mute, tied?
  What shakes here from lustre-seeded pomegranates
  Not in the great world,
  More vast and terrible?
  What is this ecstasy in form,
  This lightning

That found the lightning in my blood,
Searing my spirit's lips aghast and naked?
I am flung in the abyss of days
And the void is filled with rushing sound
From pent eternities.
I am strewn as the cypher is strewn.
A woman—a soft woman!
Our girls have hair
Like heights of night ringing with never-seen larks,
Or blindness dim with dreams.
Here is a yellow tiger gay that blinds your night.
Mane—Mane—Mane!
Your honey spilt round that small dazzling face
Shakes me to golden tremors.
I have no life at all,
Only thin golden tremors.
Light tender beast!
Your fragile gleaming wrists
Have shaken the scaled glaciers from under me,
And bored into my craft
That is now with the old dreamy Adam
With other things of dust.
LILITH. You lazy hound!   See my poor child.
            [*He turns to see* LILITH *drop the bowl and cakes and
                run to* AMAK—*who is crying, half stifled under*
                SAUL'S *huge shield*]

            [SAUL *opens his eyes*]

.   .   .   .   .   .

[*Soon after he had sent away 'The Amulet', Rosen-berg wrote to Edward Marsh (now Sir Edward Marsh): 'I hope you have not yet got my poem, "The Amulet", I've asked my sister to send you. If you get it, please don't read it, because it's the merest sketch and the best is yet to come. If I am able to carry on with it, I'll send you it in a more presentable fashion. I believe I have a good idea at bottom. It's a kind of "Rape of the Sabine Women" idea: some strange race of wanderers have settled in some wild place and are perishing out for lack of women. The prince of these explores some country near where the women are most fair. But the natives will not hear of foreign marri-ages; and he plots another Rape of the Sabines, but is trapped in the act.' The theme of lament at the prospect of extinction appears in the following poem, which exists only as a fragment without dramatic context.*]

THE TOWER OF SKULLS

Mourners

These layers of piled-up skulls,
These layers of gleaming horror—stark horror!
Ah me! Through my thin hands they touch
    my eyes.

Everywhere, everywhere is a pregnant birth,
And here in death's land is a pregnant birth.
Your own crying is less mortal
Than the amazing soul in your body.

Your own crying yon parrot takes up
And from your empty skull cries it afterwards.

Thou whose dark activities unenchanted
Days from gyrating days, suspending them
To thrust them far from sight, from the gyrating
     days
Which have gone widening on and left us here,
Cast derelicts lost for ever.

When aged flesh looks down on tender brood;
For he knows between his thin ribs' walls
The giant universe, the interminable
Panorama—synods, myths and creeds,
He knows his dust is fire and seed.

[*The following fragment was evidently an early
attempt to deal with the theme of the emotion of Tel,
prince of the decaying race, when he first sees a
woman.*]

Scene 1.   Tel on his Unicorn.   He sees a girl and
     boy in the field.   He leaves the Unicorn.

TEL'S SONG

Small dazzling face!
I shut you in my soul;
How can I perish now?

But thence a strange decay—
Your fragile gleaming wrists
Waver my days and shake my life
To golden tremors.   I have no life at all,
Only thin golden tremors

That shudder over the abyss of days
Which hedged my spirit, my spirit your
    prison walls
That shrunk like phantasms with your
    vivid beauty
Towering and widening till
The sad moonless place
Throngs with a million torches
And spears and flaming wings.

*[At one time Rosenberg planned to have the story of
the decaying race told in a myth which was to be read
by Lilith, the wife of Saul. 'Saul and Lilith', says
Rosenberg in a letter to Edward Marsh, 'are ordinary
folk into whose ordinary lives the Unicorn bursts. It
is to be a play of terror—terror of hidden things and
the fear of the supernatural.' The following scene
belongs to this conception of the play, and also develops
a theme neglected in the last complete draft—the revival
of Saul's love under the stress of his terror.]*

THE UNICORN   *

SAUL. DEALER. LILITH. TEL. AMAK.

The Unicorn

Scene. A market.

SAUL leaning against his cart in converse with DEALER.

SAUL. I saw it plain. I could have touched it.
DEALER. Against Lot's Pool you say? Strange as [the
    myth]
Of barren men, strange beasts, I lent your wife.
(Our wines are strong, the pool vapours queer shapes
And the cart's jolting made him doze and dream,

Fantasy from the strong.)
The victuals are all tied secure.   Now haste,
Before the storm breaks.   The sequel of the myth
I'll seek and bring your wife.   My greetings to her.
SAUL. The myth?   Ah yes.
Here was the usual road, the usual sky,
The same brown surging flanks, the well thewed legs
Jogging between my thoughts, the long queer ears
That seemed to hear a calling from the town.
Here was Lot's Pool, bare of the shining boys
I looked for, fishing; but it was meal-time then,
As I remembered by a hut I passed,
Then . . . I was nigh jerked from the cart
At the dead stop—like a wind it flew by—
The haughty contours of a swift white horse
And on its brows a tree, a branching [tree].
My blood froze up. . . .   Wait . . . listen!
DEALER. What shrieks? who run? why flee you, friend?
So white and mute?   I'll run with you.
SAUL. Hide me, hide me.   There, there, its horns . . .

        [*The Unicorn rushes by*]

SAUL. Is it gone?   I shake, I shake.

     [SAUL *slowly clambers into his cart, dazed*]

SAUL. G on, go on, go from this cursed [place].
It is no use if things are ordered so.
The streets are bare and strange, all seems detached.
What if I died last night, and I that ride
Is what the old place will not relinquish yet
Because Lilith now wrings her vain hands at last
By my cold form, a little colder yet,
And holds my soul back, saying, 'It cannot be.
Look look, I know his eyeballs tried to move.'

        [Lacuna]

. . . this white terror is that virgin will
Of all my unused love.   To die, to die

Before I laid my great love bare, so hidden
While she asked tenderness for alien things
Apart from my mood, or my mood despised.
I yearned for some outlet for my towering love.
My taciturn ways, cold, laconic
Like this metallic sky, scintillant.
No, no, I feel the wet drops.
How black, profoundest midnight,
There is no road or sky, yet on the brink
Noon glitters, I ride eyeless
And the rain beats and beats like endless hoofs.

[*The trapping of Tel, the chief of the decaying race,
was evidently abandoned, but some fragments refer to
the trapping of the Unicorn and apparently to its
escape.*]

TEL.   . . . Beauty,
  Music's secret soul creeping about man's senses,
  Gleaming and fading unknowable and known.
  Man yearns and woman yearns and yearning is
  Beauty and music, faith, and hope and dreams,
  Religion, love, endeavour, stability
  Of man's whole universe.

LILITH. Most secret, hidden, is my own music from me.
  Where is Saul gone?
  I hear him in the cellar with Amak.

AMAK [*off*] Father, the chain is rusty.
  Is it to chain the Unicorn?

TEL. Be wary, heart; I fear it is for me.

        [*The door is burst open and the* TRADER *rushes
        breathless in*]

TRADER. Hide, hide!   The Unicorn!   The riders!
  Our women are all taken—

105

[The Unicorn itself took the place of a woman for Tel. Something of its more general significance appears in the following rough fragment.]

LILITH. The mateless soul haunts all the elements, it wails
    In the wasting wind of obliteration.
    Surely
    The white beast is the figure of man's soul,
    Blind, passing and repassing the thing it needs
    That utters no sound, for it knows not the thing's will,
    Evil or good.
TEL. Ah Umisol, my eyes love, you have feared them
    But you have brought me hither.
    But you are barren, and man will not willingly suffer
        obliteration.
    This woman is for me—
    What Titans will those heaving breasts suckle. . . .

[It was from these and other early conceptions, fragmentary and often conflicting with each other, that Rosenberg produced the complete draft which he had hoped to use as a basis for further work on the play. His first attempt at such a draft was sent to Gordon Bottomley to read; and, when that was returned to him in camp in France, he set to work on the following re-modelling, of which also he sent a typescript to Gordon Bottomley a few days before he was killed— so few that he never learnt of its safe arrival in England.]

106

THE UNICORN

SAUL. LILITH. TEL. ENOCH
Umusol . . . The Unicorn

Scene.   A track through a woody place.   Against the hedge
is a half sunk wagon in a quagmire.   The mules stand
shivering.   Saul sits with his head between his knees.
Thunder and lightning.

SAUL.   Ah! miserable! miserable!
Is it gone . . . oooooh! that wild might of wind
Still howling in my ears . . . the glittering beast.
If I look up and see it over me
I will shrink up. . . .   I cower, I quail;
I am a shivering grass in a chill wind.
This is no mortal terror . . . spectres wail,
Stricken trunks' and beasts' spirits wail across to mine
And whirl me, strew me, pass and repass me:
Let me look up; break this unnatural fear.
Ah God! Ah God! what black thing towers towards me
Wailing. . . .
          [*A young man on horseback sweeps past crying in a
          despairing voice, 'Dora, Dora'*]
SAUL. Is there no end?   Murderers are suffered to die.
What have I done; these ghosts that seek their loves
The fearful unicorn has devoured, pass me
As if I was the road to it.
It has breathed on me, and I must reek of it.
Twice have I seen the flaring thing,
My life stormed in the wind of this.
And always wailing, wails and floats away,
The shrieks of women and the wail of men.
How chilled my spirit is, how clutched with terror,
Lilith, my Lilith
Like my hands in the membranes of my brain
To pluck your blond hair out.
I'll run to you. . . .   I totter. . . .   A wavering wall

107

Against me is the air; what pulls me back?

God! in that dizzying flash, I saw just now
Phantoms and nomads
And balls of fire pursuing
A panting streaming maenad.
What ghosts be these so white and mute.
Stay. . . .   Stay. . . .   Ah miserable . . .
That crash . . . thunder . . . no. . . .
O God it falls on me.
My brain gives way; look, look . . .

> [*The Unicorn flashes by, lit by lightning and a voice
> calls 'Umusol'*.   SAUL *sinks moaning and
> shivering against a tree*]

Ooowe. . . .   Oooowe. . . .   I sink.
A breath will lift me up and scatter me.
My name was wailed and all my tissues
Untwined and fell apart.

Sick. . . .   Sick. . . .   I will lie down and die.   How
    can I die?
Kind lightning, sweetest lightning, cleave me through
Lift up these shreds of being and mix me with
This wind, this darkness.
I'll strive once more.   See how the wheels are sunk
Right to the axle. . . .   Ah impotent puny me. . . .
Vain.   Futile.
Hi hi hi hi, is there no man about?
Who would be wandering in a storm like this?—
Hark . . . was that a human voice?
Sh . . . when that crash ceases.
Like laughter . . . like laughter,
Sure that was laughter . . . just the laughter of ours.
Hi hi hi hi hi hi. . . .
My voice fears me.
God cover my eyes.

[*The Unicorn rushes by and when he looks up again,
his hair stands up.   A naked black giant stands
there and signs for* SAUL'S *hand.   Mechani-
cally as in a trance,* SAUL *gives his hand and
together they heave and lift the wheels.   The
mules suddenly start;* SAUL *is lifted into the
cart and the black drives.   The exertion has
revived* SAUL *who is thinking of the warm
humanlike grasp of the hand in his.*]

SAUL. Why quails my heart?   God riding with
A mortal would absorb him.
He touched my hand, here is my hand the same.
Sure I am whirled in some dark fantasy—
A dizzying cloven wink, the beast, the black,
And I ride now . . . ride, ride, the way I know
That rushing terror. . . .   I shudder yet.
The haughty contours of a swift white horse
And on its brows a tree, a branching tree,
And on its back a golden girl bound fast.
It glittered by
And all the phantoms wailing.
Then sudden, here I ride.
His monstrous posture, why his neck's turn
Were our thews' adventures; some Amazon's son
        doubtless
From the dark countries.   Can it be
The storm spirit, storm's pilot
With all the heaving débris of Noah's sunken days
Dragged on his loins.
What have I lived and agonised today, today.
It seems long centuries since I went to the town
For our week's victuals, I saw the beast
And rode into the town a shaken ghost,
Not Saul at all, but something that was Saul,
And saw folk wailing; and men that could not
        weep.
And my heart utterance was Lilith,

109

Whose face seemed cast in faded centuries
While the beast was rushing back towards her,
Sweeping past me, leaving me so with the years.
Mere human travail never broke my spirit
Only my throat to impatient blasphemies.
But God's unthinkable imagination
Invents new tortures for nature
Whose wisdom falters here.
No used experience can make aware
The imminent unknowable.
Sudden destruction
Till the stricken soul wails in anguish
Torn here and there.
Man could see and live never believed.
I ride. . . .   I ride . . . thunder crowned
In the shelter of a glis'ning chanting giant.
What flaring chant the storm's undertones,
Full of wild yearning,
And makes me think of Lilith
And that swift beast, it went that way.
My house my blood all lean to its weird flight.
But Lilith will be sleeping . . . ah miss my Lilith.
Swifter my mules swifter
Destroy the space . . . transport me instantly
For my soul yearns and fears.

TEL. How his voice fears. . . .   If I strove utterance
  What fear would be in mine.
  I saw her. . . .   I fled . . . he brings me back.
  Umusol . . . a golden mane shall mingle with your
      horns
  Before the storm shall cease.

SAUL. Yonder, my house is yonder.
  I feared to see it vanished
  On the ground from Lilith.

TEL. The powered storm means such devastation.

110

(I dread to enter, yet my soul hungers so intense).

> [SAUL *springs from the cart and hurries into the room where* LILITH *sits white and terror stricken, wringing her hands*]

LILITH. Pity me.   Where is Saul. . . .
Do not touch me.
SAUL. Lilith dear, look up, it is me.
LILITH. Saul, oh Saul, do not go away.
Who is that?

> [SAUL *kisses her*]

SAUL. How frightened you are.
See where I sunk in the mire, the mud . . .
His was the healing hand.
Lilith your viol
To force this gloom away even while I dry
In the inner chamber.
I am dank and tired.
LILITH. Saul do not leave me,
I dread to look up and see again
Two balls of fire casement glaring. . . .
SAUL. This is some fantasy: play music till I come.

> [TEL *crouches in the shadow and she turns to take the viol down*]

LILITH. The roots of a torn universe are wrenched,
See the bent trees like nests of derelicts in ocean
That beats upon this ark.
TEL. Unearthly accents float amid the howling storm.
Her mouth moves . . . is it thence. . . .
Secret Mother of my orphan spirit
Who art thou?
LILITH. I think he speaks, this howling storm sheets out
all so.
I'll play and ease my heavy heart.
TEL. Was that the lightning?
Those fragile gleaming wrists untangle me,
Those looks tread out my soul.

Somewhere I know those looks, I lost it somewhere.

[LILITH *draws nearer and sings softly*]

LILITH. Beauty is music's secret soul,
Creeping about man's senses.
He cannot hold it or know it ever,
But yearns and yearns to hold it once.
Ah! when he yearns not shall he not wither?
For music then will have no place
In the world's ear, but mix in windless darkness.

TEL. Am I gone blind?
I swim in a white haze.
What shakes my life to golden tremors . . .?
I have no life at all. . . . I am a crazed shadow
From a golden body
That melts my iron flesh, I flow from it.
I know the haze, the light,
I am a shuddering pulse
Hung over the abyss. I shall look up
Even if I fall, fall, fall, fall forever,
I faint, tremble.

LILITH. Still the rain beats and beats.

[TEL *looks up furtively, then prostrates himself*]

TEL. Ah woe, ah woe. [*He sobs*]

LILITH. Has lightning turned his brain?
Is this a maniac? Saul, Saul.

TEL. Hear me, hear me.
Do I speak, or think I speak,
I am so faint. . . . Wait,
Let my dazed blood resolve itself to words.
Where have I strayed . . . incomprehensible . . .
Yet here . . . somewhere
An instant flashes a large face of dusk
Like heights of night ringing with unseen larks
Or blindness dim with dreams.
I hear a low voice . . . a crooning. . . .
Some whisperings, shadows vast,

112

A crying through the forest, wailing.
Behind impassable places
Whose air was never warmed by a woman's lips
Bestial man shapes ride dark impulses
Through roots in the bleak blood, then hide
In shuddering light from their self loathing.
They fade in arid light—
Beings unnatured by their craving, for they know
Obliteration's spectre.   They are few.
They wail their souls for continuity,
And bow their heads and knock their breasts before
The many mummies whose wail in dust is more
Than these who cry, their brothers who loiter yet.
Great beasts' and small beasts' eyes have place
As eyes of women to their hopeless eyes
That hunt in bleakness for the dread might,
The incarnate female soul of generation.
The daughters of any clime are not imagined
Even of their occult ears, senses profound,
For their corporeal ears and baby senses
Were borne for gentle voices and gentle forms
By men misused flying from misuse
Who gave them suck even from their narrow breasts
Only for this, that they should wither
That they should be as an uttered sound in the wind.
> [*He sees* SAUL'S *smouldering eyes in the doorway.*
> *It rouses him*]
By now my men have raided the city,
I heard a far shrieking.
LILITH. This is most piteous, most fearful,
I fear him, his hungry eyes
Burn into me, like those balls of fire.
TEL. There is a tower of skulls,
Where birds make nests
And staring beasts stand by with many flocks
And man looks on with hopeless eyes . . .
LILITH. O horrible, I hear Saul rattle those chains in the cellar.

113

TEL. What clanking chains?
When a man's brains crack with longing
We chain him to some slender beast to breed.
LILITH. Tell me, tell me, who took my cousin Dora,
Oh God those balls of fire . . .
Are you men . . . ? tell me.
TEL. Marvellous creature.
Night tender beast.
Has the storm passed into me,
What ecstasy, what lightning
Has touched the lightning in my blood.
Voluptuous
Crude vast terrible hunger overpowers . . .
A gap . . . a yawning . . .
My blood knocks . . . inarticulate to make you under-
stand,
To shut you in itself
Uncontrollable. [*He stretches his arms out*]
Small dazzling face I shut you in my soul—
    [*She shrieks. SAUL appears, looking about dazed,
    holding an iron chain; while the door is burst
    open and ENOCH bursts in. He springs on
    TEL*]
ENOCH. Where is my Dora, where?
Pity, rider of the Unicorn.
TEL. Yonder.
    [*Through the casement they see riding under the
    rainbow a black naked host on various animals,
    the Unicorn leading. A woman is clasped on
    every one, some are frantic, others white or un-
    conscious, some nestle laughing. ENOCH with
    madness in his eyes leaps through the casement
    and disappears with a splash in the well.
    SAUL leaps after him shouting 'The Unicorn'.
    TEL places the unconscious LILITH on the Unicorn
    and they all ride away*]

114

EARLIER POEMS
UNPUBLISHED BY ROSENBERG
1914-1915

SIGNIFICANCE *

The cunning moment curves its claws
Round the body of our curious wish,
But push a shoulder through its straitened
    laws—
Then are you hooked to wriggle like a fish.

Lean in high middle 'twixt two tapering points,
Yet rocks and undulations control
The agile brain, the limber joints
The sinews of the soul.

Chaos that coincides, form that refutes all
    sway,
Shapes to the eye quite other to the touch,
All twisted things continue to our clay
Like added limbs and hair dispreaded over-
    much.

And after it draws in its claws
The rocks and unquiet sink to a flat ground.
Then follow desert hours, the vacuous pause
Till some mad indignation unleashes the hound.

And those flat hours and dead unseeing things
Cower and crowd and burrow for us to use,
Where sundry gapings spurn and preparing
    wings—
And O! our hands would use all ere we lose.

1915

WEDDED *

[II]

The knotted moment that untwists
Into the narrow laws of love,
Its ends are rolled round our four wrists
That once could stretch and rove.

See our confinèd fingers stray
O'er delicate fibres that recoil,
And blushing hints as cold as clay;
Love is tired after toil.

But hush! two twin moods meet in air;
Two spirits of one gendered thought.
Our chained hands loosened everywhere
Kindness like death's have caught.

THE MIRROR *

It glimmers like a wakeful lake in the dark narrowing
    room.
Like drowning vague branches in its depth floats the
    gloom,
The night shall shudder at its face by gleams of pallid
    light
Whose hands build the broader day to break the husk of
    night.

No shade shall waver there when your shadowless soul
    shall pass,
The green shakes not the air when your spirit drinks the
    grass,
So in its plashless water falls, so dumbly lies therein
A fervid rose whose fragrance sweet lies hidden and shut
    within.

Only in these bruised words the glass dim-showing my
    spirit's face,
Only a little colour from a fire I could not trace,
To glimmer through eternal days like an enchanted rose,
The potent dreamings of whose scent are wizard-locked
    beneath its glows.

DUSK AND THE MIRROR *

Where the room seems ponder-
    ing,
Shadowy hovering,
Pictured walls and dove-dim
    ceiling,
Edgeless, lost and spectral,
In a quaint half farewell
Away the things familiar fall
In some limbo to a spell.
Mutation of slipped moment
When nothing and solid is blent.
O! dusk palpitant!
Prank fantastical!
You hide and steal from
    morning
What you give back from
    hiding,
You prank before the dawning
And run from her frail chiding,
And all my household Gods
When he who worships nods
You tweak and pinch and hide
And dabble under your side
To drop upon the shores
Of an old tomorrow
Shut with the same old doors
Of sleep and shame and sorrow.

But naked you have left
One jewel, dripping still
From plundering plashless
    fingers.
Lying in a cleft
Of your own surging-bosomed
    hill,

It dreams of dreams bereft
And warm dishevelled singers,
Safe from your placeless will.

Or you are like a tree now,
And that is like a lake,
Sinister to thee now
Its glimmer is awake.
Like vague undrowning boughs
Above the pool
You float your gloom in its low
    light
Where Narcissian augurs browse,
Dreaming from its cool
Apparition a fear;
Behind the wall of hours you
    hear
The tread of the arch light.

1915

120

'WHO LOSES THE HOUR OF THE WIND?'   *

Who loses the hour of the wind
Where the outer silence swings?
But frail—but pale are the things
We seek and the seekers blind.
They seek us on broken wings.

No cold kiss blown from the surge
Of the dark tides of the night.
We sleep and blind is their flight
The dreams of whose kisses urge
The soul to endure its plight.

Blown words, whose root is the brain,
Live over your ruined root.
For other mouths is the fruit
And the songs so rich with pain
Of a splendour whose lips were mute.

1915

'PAST DAYS ARE HIEROGLYPHS' *

Past days are hieroglyphs
Scrawled behind the brows
Scarred deep with iron blows,
Upon the thundered tree
Of memory.

Marvellous mad beliefs
(To believe that you believed!),
Plain and time-unthieved,
Scratched and scrawled on the tree
Of memory.

Time, good graver of griefs,
Those words sapped with my soul,
That I read as of old and whole,
What eye in the world shall see
On this covered tree?

1915

BEAUTY *

[II]

Far and near, and now, from never,
My calm beauty burns for ever,
Through the forests deep and old
Which loose their miser secrets hold,
Unto the fountains of the sky,
Whose showers of radiant melody
Delight the laughter-burdened ways,
And dress the hours to light the days,
While hand in hand they reel their round;
For the burning bush is found.
Joy has blossomed, joy has burst;
And earth's parched lips and dewy thirst
Have found a shroud of summer mirth,
And Eden covers all the earth
Whose lips love's kisses did anoint,
And straight our ashes fell away.
Our lives are now a burning point,
And faded are their walls of clay,
Purged of the flames that loved the wind
Is the pure glow that has not sinned.

1914

ON RECEIVING NEWS OF THE WAR

Snow is a strange white word.
No ice or frost
Has asked of bud or bird
For Winter's cost.

Yet ice and frost and snow
From earth to sky
This Summer land doth know.
No man knows why.

In all men's hearts it is.
Some spirit old
Hath turned with malign kiss
Our lives to mould.

Red fangs have torn His face.
God's blood is shed.
He mourns from His lone place
His children dead.

O! ancient crimson curse!
Corrode, consume.
Give back this universe
Its pristine bloom.

Cape Town.   1914

AUGURIES *

Fading fire that does not fade,
Only changing its nest,
Sky-blown words of cloudlike breath
Live in another sky.
Days that are scrawled hieroglyphs
On thunder-stricken barks,
First our souls have plucked the fruit.
Here are Time's granaries.
Were we not fed of summer, but warmth
      and summer sang to us.
Has my soul plucked all the fruit?
Not all the fruit that hung thereon—
The trees whose barks were pictured days.
One waits somewhere for me
Holding fresh the fruit I left,
And I hold fruit for one.
What screen hid us gathering
And lied unto our thirst,
While two faces looked singly to the moon?
But the moon was secret and chill.

Will my eyes know the fruit I left?
Will her eyes know her own?
This broken stem will surely know
And leap unto its leaf.
No blossom bursts before its time
No angel passes by the door,
But from old Chaos shoots the bough
While we grow ripe for heaven.

1914

BEAUTY *

[I]

An angel's chastity
Unfretted by an earthly angel's
    lures.
The occult lamp of beauty
Which holds? Is truth? Whose
    spreaded wing endures?

Say—beauty springs and grows
From the flushed night of the
    nun solitude
And the deep spirit's throes.
Unconscious as in Eden—chaste
    and nude.

His self-appointed aim,
Whose bloodless brows bloom with
    austere delight,
O'er his entombèd fame,
Whose ghost, an unseen glory,
    walks in hidden light.

Her sire and her lover.
He burns the world to gloat on the
    bright flame,
Her absence doth him cover.
Her silence is a voice that calls
    his name.

From the womb's antechambers
He, list'ning, moves through life's
    wide presence-hall,
Blindly its turret clambers,
Then searches his own soul for the
    flying bacchanal.

Is she an earthly care
Moulding our needs unto her
    gracious ends,
Making the rough world fair,
With softer meanings than its
    rude speech lends?

               1914

'I AM THE BLOOD'   *

I am the blood
Streaming the veins of sweet-
    ness; sharp and sweet,
Beauty has pricked the live
    veins of my soul
And sucked all being in.

I am the air
Prowling the room of beauty,
    climbing her soft
Walls of surmise, her ceilings
    that close in.
She breathes me as her breath.

I am the death
Whose monument is beauty,
    and forever,
Although I lie unshrouded
    in life's tomb,
She is my cenotaph.

'SUMMER'S LIPS ARE AGLOW' *

Summer's lips are aglow, afresh
For our old lips to kiss,
The tingling of the flesh
Makes life aware of this.

Whose eyes are wild with love?
Whose hair a blowing flame
I feel around and above
Laughing my dreams to shame?

My dreams like stars gone out
Were blossoms for your day;
Red flower of mine I will shout,
I have put my dreams away.

                    1914–1915

'I HAVE LIVED IN THE UNDERWORLD
TOO LONG'   *

I have lived in the underworld too long
For you, O creature of light,
To hear without terror the dark spirit's song
And unmoved hear what moves in night.

I am a spirit that yours has found
Strange, undelightful, obscure,
Created by some other God, and bound
In terrible darkness impure.

Creature of light and happiness,
Deeper the darkness when you
With your bright terror eddying the distress
Grazed the dark waves and shivering further
        flew.

                    1914

128

'HER FABLED MOUTH'   *

Her fabled mouth, love hath from fables made.
She tells the same old marvels and sweet stories.
Chaos within her eyes his jewels laid.
Our lips and eyes dig up the antique glories.

The wonder of her heavy coloured hair
Still richly wears the hues of faded Eden;
There, where primeval dream hath made its lair,
Joy subtly smiles, in his arms sorrow hidden.

O! as her eyes grow wide and starlight wanes,
Wanes from our hearts that grow into her
    splendour,
We melt with wronging of love's fabled pains,
Her eyes so kind, her bosom white and tender.

1914

'A BIRD TRILLING ITS GAY HEART OUT'   *

A bird trilling its gay heart out
Made my idle heart a cage for it
Just as the sunlight makes a cage
Of the lampless world its song has
    lit.

I was half happy and half vexed
Because the song flew in unasked
Just as the dark might angry be
If sudden light her face unmasked.

I could not shut my spirit's doors
I was so naked and alone,
I could not hide and it saw that
I would not to myself have shown.

1914

THE FEMALE GOD

We curl into your eyes—
They drink our fires and have never
    drained.
In the fierce forest of your hair
Our desires beat blindly for their treasure.

In your eyes' subtle pit,
Far down, glimmer our souls.
And your hair like massive forest trees
Shadows our pulses, overtired and dumb.

Like a candle lost in an electric glare
Our spirits tread your eyes' infinities.
In the wrecking waves of your tumultuous
    locks
Do you not hear the moaning of our pulses?

Queen! Goddess! Animal!
In sleep do your dreams battle with our
    souls?
When your hair is spread like a lover on the
    pillow
Do not our jealous pulses wake between?

You have dethroned the ancient God,
You have usurped his Sabbath, his common
    days,
Yea! every moment is delivered to you,
Our Temple, our Eternal, our one God.

Our souls have passed into your eyes,
Our days into your hair,
And you, our rose-deaf prison, are very
    pleased with the world,
Your world.

DAWN

O tender first cold flush of rose,
O budded dawn, wake dreamily;
Your dim lips as your lids unclose
Murmur your own sad threnody.
O as the soft and frail lights break
Upon your eyelids, and your eyes
Wider and wider grow and wake,
The old pale glory dies.

And then as sleep lies down to sleep
And all her dreams lie somewhere dead,
(While naked day digs goldly deep
For light to lie uncoverèd),
Your own ghost fades with dream-
    ghosts there,
Our lorn eyes see, mid glimmering
    lips,
Pass through the haunted dream-
    moved air,
Slowly, their laden ships.

1914

'WHAT IF I WEAR YOUR BEAUTY' *

What if I wear your beauty as this present
Wears infinite aeons yet is only now?
The spirit opens but to receive,
Close hid, nought yet departing—
But the world's gaze lessens love.

O softer pearl whose iridescent fountain
Hath been my sky, my sun, my stream of
    light
From the first dazzling daystream, the
    enfolden
Sweet thirst, a mother prattle
To a new babbled birth.

I like an insect beautiful wings have gotten,
Shed from you.   Let me hide, O like a
    vessel
That you have marvel-laden, burdened
With new rich fears of pirates
I droop dark pendulous sails.

1914

NIGHT   *

With sleek lascivious velvety caresses
The nestling hair of night strays on my cheeks.
My heart is full of brimless fervid fancies
Ardent to hear the imperious word she speaks.

O purple-hued—O glimmering mouth that
    trembles,
O monstrous dusky shoulders lost above,
Wrapt in bleak robes of smoke from eye, star
    embers,
You smouldering pyres of flaming aeons of love.

The straining lusts of strenuous amorists,
Smoking from crimson altars of their hearts,
In burning mists are shed upon my dreaming.

Relax—relax.   I have not strength to withstand
    thee.
My soul will not recoil, so full of thee.
Thy loathsomeness and beauty fill my hunger
O! splendid, thy lithe fingers gripping me.

Naked and glorious like a shining temple
I fill with adorations, fervent psalm,
Anoint with honey of kisses, while thy bosom
Throbs music to my unprofaning palm.

See how thy breasts, those two white grapes of
    passion,
Look mixed in mine, like globed fruit mixed
    with leaves.
Lo! where I press, what crimson stains come
    leaping,
Bright juice of inexhaustible dreams lust weaves.

'MY SOUL IS ROBBED' *

[I]

My soul is robbed by your most treacherous eyes
Treading its intricate infinities.
Some pale light hidden in light and felt to stir
In listening pulse, an audible wonder
Delighting me with my immortal loss;
While you stay in its place, rich robbers, that is
    dross.
Wine of the Almighty who got drunk with thee.
(The reason sin—God slumbering then—flew
    free.)
Alas! if God thus, what will hap to me?
Ah! even now drunken while your sweet light
    beams,
You, far as Heaven, I am drunk on my dreams.
Not yet, that glance engendered ecstasy,
That subtle, unspaced, mutual intimacy,
Whereby two spirits of one thought commune,
Like separate instruments that play one tune.
The music of my playing is lost in thine.
Does the sun see when noonday torches shine?
Mine is not yours though you have stolen mine.
Beautiful thieves, I cannot captive ye,
Being so bound even as ye rifle me.
My limbs that moved in trembling innocence
You harden to knowledge of experience
Till honour rings upon the ear as crime.

THE EXILE   *

A northern spray in an all human speech
To this same torrid heart may somewhat reach,
Although its root, its mother tree
Is in the North.
But O! to its cold heart, and fervid eyes,
It sojourns in another's paradise,
A loveliness its alien eyes might see
Could its own roots go forth.

O! dried-up waters of deep hungering love!
Far, far, the springs that fed you from above,
And brimmed the wells of happiness
With new delight.
Blinding ourselves to rob another's sun
Only its scorching glory have we won,
And left our own homes in bleak wintriness
Moaning our sunward flight.

Here, where the craggy mountains edge the skies,
Whose profound spaces stare to our vain eyes;
Where our thoughts hang, and theirs, who yearn
To know our speech.
O! what winged airs soothe the sharp mountains'
    brow?
From peak to peak with messages they go,
Withering our peering thoughts that crowd to
    learn
Words from that distant beach.

Sacred, voluptuous hollows deep
Where the unlifted shadows sleep
Beneath inviolate mouth and chin.
What virginal woven mystery
Guarding some pleadful spiritual sin,
So hard to traffic with or flee,
Lies in your chaste impurity?

Warm, fleshly chambers of delights,
Whose lamps are we, our days and nights.
Where our thoughts nestle, our lithe limbs
Frenzied exult till vision swims
In fierce delicious agonies;
And the crushed life, bruised through and
        through,
Ebbs out, trophy no spirit slew,
While molten sweetest pains enmesh
The life sucked by entwining flesh.

O rosy radiance incarnate,
O glowing glory of heaven-dreamt flesh,
O seraph-barred resplendent gate
Of paradisal meadows fresh.
O read—read what my pale mouth tells.
God! could that mouth be but the air
To kiss your chasteness everywhere
Bound with lust's shrivelling manacles!

As weary water dreams of land
While waves roll back and leave wet sand,
Their white tongues fawning on its breast,
But turns it to the thing that prest,
Though my thoughts drown you sweet,
        and cover,
Your shape in me is my mad lover.

'I KNOW YOU GOLDEN'   *

I know you golden
As summer and pale
As the clinging sweetness
Of marvels frail.

A touch of fire,
A loitering thrill,
My dancing spirit
Has passed the will.

And love and living
And Time and space—
My naked spirit
Hath seen its face.

GIRL'S SONG   *

The pigmy skies cover
No mood in my eyes,
The flat earth foams over
My pallor's moonrise.
Thin branches like whips
Whiten the skies
To gibbous lips
Calling for my mad lover.

What is his knowledge
Knowing not this?
I'll send him a message,
My life in a kiss.
Why is he mad?
I hold fires for him, bliss
He has not had
And dare not aspire.

1914–1915

* ©   137

FAR AWAY

By what pale light or moon-pale shore
Drifts my soul in lonely flight?
Regions God had floated o'er
Ere He touched the world with light?

Not in Heaven and not in earth
Is this water, is this moon;
For there is no starry birth,
And no dawning and no noon.

Far away—O far away,
Mist-born—dewy vapours rise
From the dim gates of the day
Far below in earthly skies.

'HAVE WE SAILED AND HAVE WE WANDERED'   *

Have we sailed and have we wandered,
Still beyond, the hills are blue.
Have we spent and have we squandered,
What's before us still is new.

See the foam of unheard waters
And the gleam of hidden skies,
Footsteps of Eve's whiter daughters
Flash between our dreaming eyes.

Soundless waning to the spirit,
Still—O still the hills are blue,
Ever and yet never near it,
There where our far childhood grew.

138

'WISTFULLY IN PALLID SPLENDOUR' *

Wistfully in pallid splendour
Drifts the lonely infinite,
A wan perfume vague and tender,
Dim with feet of fragile light.

Drifts so lightly through the spirit,
Breathes the torch of dreams astir
Till what promised lands lie near it
Wavering are betrayed to her.

Ghostly foam of unheard waters,
And the gleam of hidden skies,
Footsteps of Eve's whiter daughters
Tremble to our dreaming eyes.

O! sad wraith of joy lips parted,
Hearing not a word they say—
Even my dreams make broken-hearted
And their beauty falls away.

THE POET *

[III]

At my eyes' anchoring levels
The pigmy skies foam over
The flat earth our senses see;
A vapour my lips might stir—
The heat of my breath might
    wither.
Strong unfed eyes, so baffled!
Yon bright and moving vapour
In a moment fades.

The beamy air, the roofless
    silence;
The smoke-throated, man-
    thundered street,
Die to an essence, a love spirit,
Which my life feels to stir;
Some subtle compound wrought
By no wonder-list'ning sleep.
All things that, brooding, are still,
Speak to me, untwist and twine
The shifting links of conscious-
    ness,
Speak to the all-eyed soul
And tread its intricate infinities,
Pass through the ward of our immured
    immensity
Into the secret God, behind the
    mask of man.

1914

AT NIGHT

Crazed shadow, from no golden body
That I can see, embraces me warm;
All is purple and closed
Round by night's arm.

A brilliance wings from dark-lit voices,
Wild lost voices of shadows white.
See the long houses lean
To the weird flight.

Star-amorous things that wake at sleep-
     time
(Because the sun spreads wide like a
     tree
With no good fruit for them)
Thrill secrecy.

Pale horses ride before the morning
The secret roots of the sun to tread,
With hoofs shod with venom
And ageless dread,

To breathe on burning emerald grasses,
And opalescent dews of the day,
And poison at the core
What smiles may stray.

1914

Invisible ancient enemy of mine,
My house's foe,
To rich my pride with wrongful suffering,
Your vengeful gain—
Coward and striker in the pit lined dark—
Lie to my friends,
Feed the world's jealousy and pamper woe.

When I had bowed
I felt your smile, when my large spirit
    groaned
And hid its fire
Because another spirit leaned on it,
I knew you near.

O that the tortured spirit could amass
All the world's pains,
How I would cheat you, leaving none for life,
You would recount
All you have piled on me, self-tortured count
Through all eternity.

1914

OF ANY OLD MAN

Wreck not the ageing heart of quietness
With alien uproar and rude jolly cries,
Which (satyr-like to a mild maiden's pride)
Ripen not wisdom but a large recoil.
Give them their withered peace, their trial
    grave,
Their past youth's three-scored shadowy
    effigy.
Mock them not with your ripened turbulence,
Their frost-mailed petulance with your torrid
    wrath,
When, edging your boisterous thunders,
    shivers one word
(Pap to their senile sneering, drug to truth,
The feignèd rampart of bleak ignorance)
'Experience'—crown of naked majesties,
That tells us naught we know not, but con-
    firms.
O think, you reverend shadowy austere,
Your Christ's youth was not ended when
    he died.

1914

O heart, home of high purposes,
O hand with craft and skill,
Say, why this meagre dalliance
To do such greatness ill?

Marshal the flame-winged legions, yours,—
The thunder and the beauty;
Sweeten these sunsoiled days of ours,
We need your wizard duty.

Our parched lips yearn for music yet.
Find us some gate in air
To leave our world-stained lives behind,
And live a life more fair.

The vagrant clouds are alive with light
When the sun shines and sings,
When the wind blows they race in flight
So happy in their wings.

Help us, the helpless, breathe thy breath,
Show us new flowers, new ways to live,
Thy glory thaw our lips of death,
To you your feel of power we'll give.

AT SEA-POINT   *

Let the earth crumble away,
The heavens fade like a breath,
The sea go up in a cloud,
And its hills be given to death.

For the roots of the earth are old,
And the pillars of heaven are
      tired.
The hands that the sea enfold
Have seen a new desired.

All things upon my sense
Are wasted spaces dull,
Since one shape passed like a
      song
Let God all things annul.

A lie with its heart hidden
Is that cruel wall of air
That held her there unbidden,
Who comes not at my prayer.

Gone, who yet never came.
There is the breathing sea,
And the shining skies are the
      same,
But they lie—they lie to me.

For she stood with the sea below,
Between the sky and the sea,
She flew ere my soul was aware,
But left this thirst in me.

EARLIER POEMS

1913

ON A LADY SINGING

She bade us listen to the singing lark
In tones far sweeter than its own.
For fear that she should cease and
    leave us dark
We built the bird a feignèd throne,
Shrined in her gracious glory-giving
    ways
From sceptred hands of starred
    humility—
Praising herself the more in giving
    praise
To music less than she.

'AS A SWORD IN THE SUN—'

As a sword in the sun—
A glory calling a glory—
Our eyes seeing it run
Capture its gleam for our story.

Singer, marvellous gleam
Dancing in splendid light,
Here you have brought us our
    dream—
Ah, but its stay is its flight!

SONG *

A silver rose to show
Is your sweet face,
And like the heavens' white
    brow,
Sometime God's battle-place,
Your blood is quiet now.

Your body is a star
Unto my thought.
But stars are not too far
And can be caught—
Small pools their prisons are.

SPRING

I walk and I wonder
To hear the birds sing—
Without you my lady
How can there be Spring?
I see the pink blossoms
That slept for a year,
But who could have woke
    them
While you were not near?

Birds sing to the blossoms,
Blind, dreaming your pink;
These blush to the songsters,
Your music they think.
So well had you taught them
To look and to sing,
Your bloom and your music,
The ways of the Spring.

* ©   150

'A WARM THOUGHT FLICKERS' *

A warm thought flickers
An idle ray—
Being is one blush at root.

For the hours' ungentle doom
Where one forsaking face
Hides ever—hides for our sighing
Is a hard bright leaf over clover
And bee-bitten shade.

What moons have hidden
Their month-long shine,
What buds uncover
And plead in vain,
While one opaque thought
     wearies
The weary lids of grief?

One thought too heavy
For words to bear,
For lips too tired
To curl to them.

O, be these men and women
That pass and cry like blowing
    flakes,
Seeking the parent cloud,
Seeking the parent sea?
Or like famished flames that fly
On a separate root of fire
Far from the nurturing furnace.
Or like scent from the flower
That hovers in doubt afar,
Or the colour of grasses
That flies to the spirit and
    spreads.

Are these things your dreams
That I too can watch?
When I dream my dreams
Do you see them too?
When the ghosts depart
Can you follow them,
Though I see them not?

TWILIGHT *

[III]

A sumptuous splendour of leaves
Murmurously fanning the evening heaven;
And I hear
In the soft living grey shadows,
In the brooding evanescent atmo-
    sphere,
The voice of impatient night.

The splendour shall vanish in a
    vaster splendour;
Its own identity shall lose itself,
And the golden glory of day
Give birth to the lambent face of
    the twilight,
And she shall grow into a vast
    enormous pearl maiden
Whose velvet tresses shall envelop the
    world—
Night.

THE BLIND GOD

Streaked with immortal blasphemies,
Betwixt twin eternities
Shaper of mortal destinies
Sits in that limbo of dreamless sleep,
Some nothing that hath shadows deep.

The world is only a small pool
In the meadows of Eternity,
And the wise man and the fool
In its depths like fishes lie.
When an angel drops a rod
And he draws you to the sky
Will you bear to meet your God
You have streaked with blasphemy?

'WALK YOU IN MUSIC, LIGHT OR NIGHT'   *

Walk you in music, light or night,
Spelled on your brows, plain to men's
    sight
Is death and darkness written clear.
God only can neither read nor hear.

Ah men, ye are so skilled to write
This doom so dark in letters bright.
But how can God read human fear
Who cannot dry a human tear?

A CARELESS HEART

A little breath can make a prayer,
A little wind can take it
And turn it back again to air:
Then say, why should you make it?

An ardent thought can make a word,
A little ear can hear it,
A careless heart forget it heard:
Then why keep ever near it?

THE POET   *

[II]

He takes the glory from the gold
For consecration of the mould,
He strains his ears to the clouds' lips,
He sings the song they sang to him
And his brow dips
In amber that the seraphim
Have held for him and hold.

So shut in are our lives, so still,
That we see not of good or ill—
A dead world since ourselves are dead.
Till he, the master, speaks and lo!
The dead world's shed,
Strange winds, new skies and rivers flow
Illumined from the hill.

* ©   155

A QUESTION

What if you shut your eyes and look,
Yea, look with all the spirit's eyes,
While mystic unrevealèd skies
Unfold like pages of a book

Wherein new scenes of wonder rare
Are imaged, till the sense deceives
Itself, and what it sees believes—
Even what the soul has pictured there?

APPARITION   *

From her hair's unfelt gold
My days are twined,
As the moon weaves pale daughters
Her hands may never fold.

Her eyes are hidden pools
Where my soul lies
Glimmering in their waters
Like faint and troubled skies.

Dream pure, her body's grace,
A streaming light,
Scatters delicious fire
Upon my limbs and face.

'GLORY OF HUELESS SKIES' *

Glory of hueless skies,
What pallid splendour flies
Like visible music touched
From the lute of our eyes.

The stars are sick and white,
Old in the morning light;
Like genius in a rabble
The obscure mars their might.

The forest of the world,
Lights scattering hands have uphurled,
The branches of thought are driven
The vapours of act are uncurled.

Deed against strenuous deed,
Dark seed choking the seed,
The impulses blind that blacken
The ways of life's rough need.

Mountain and man and beast,
Live flower and leaf diseased
Riot or revel in quiet
At the broad day's feast.

CREATION

As the pregnant womb of night
Thrills with imprisoned light,
Misty, nebulous-born,
Growing deeper into her morn,
So man, with no sudden stride,
Bloomed into pride.

In the womb of the All-spirit
The universe lay; the will
Blind, an atom, lay still.
The pulse of matter
Obeyed in awe
And strove to flatter
The rhythmic law.
But the will grew; nature feared,
And cast off the child she reared,
Now her rival, instinct-led,
With her own powers impregnated.

Brain and heart, blood-fervid flowers,
Creation is each act of yours.
Your roots are God, the pauseless cause,
But your boughs sway to self-windy laws.
Perception is no dreamy birth
And magnifies transfigured earth.
With each new light, our eyes receive
A larger power to perceive.

If we could unveil our eyes,
Become as wise as the All-wise,
No love would be, no mystery:
Love and joy dwell in infinity.
Love begets love; reaching highest
We find a higher still, unseen
From where we stood to reach the first;

Moses must die to live in Christ,
The seed be buried to live to green.
Perfection must begin from worst.
Christ perceives a larger reachless love,
More full, and grows to reach thereof.
The green plant yearns for its yellow fruit.
Perfection always is a root,
And joy a motion that doth feed
Itself on light of its own speed,
And round its radiant circle runs,
Creating and devouring suns.

Thus human hunger nourisheth
The plan terrific—true design—
Makes music with the bones of death,
And soul knows soul to shine.
What foolish lips first framed 'I sin'?
The virgin spirit grows within
To stature its eyes know to fail.
And all its edges weaken and pale
Where the flesh merges and is one;
A chalice of light for stagnation
To drink, but where no dust can come
Till the glass shatters and light is dumb.
Soul grows in freedom natural.
When in wild growths eventual
Its light casts shadow on other light,
All cry 'That spirit is not white'.
As when God strides through the wrack
        of skies,
The plunging seas welcome paradise,
They say not 'This dark period
Sheweth our bitter wrong to God',
But revel in a dark delight,
And day is sweet and night is bright.
The jewelled green laughs myriadly.

The yearning pits swing and draw down
The rainbow-splintered mountains thrown
By wrestling giants beneath the sea.

An emanation like a voice
Spreads up, the spirits of our joys.
The sky receives it like an ear
Bent o'er the throbbing atmosphere.
Our thoughts like endless waterfalls
Are fed—to fill life's palace halls
Until the golden gates do close
On endless gardens of repose.
A sun, long set, again shall rise,
Bloom in annihilation's skies
Strong—strong—past ruin to endure,
More lost than bliss—than life more sure.
This universe shall be to me
Millions of years beneath the sea
Cast from my rock of changelessness,
The centre of eternity.
And uncreated nothingness
Found, what creation laboured for
The ultimate silence—Ah, no more
A happy fool in paradise,
But finite—wise as the All-wise.

AS A BESIEGED CITY   *

In the hushed pregnancy
And gleaming of hope,
When a joy's infancy
Fills our stars' horoscope,
Flowering like a mist
Heaven-mixed but light-unkist,
The soul is mixed in anguish,
For joy has not yet burst.

Expectant is the fear—
O! why the doubt?
Surely our friends are near,
And the strong foe cast out.
Ah! but if we are dead
In their loving fears, and shed
The tears for us in anguish,
And they turn from gates not burst.

TWILIGHT *

[II]

Mist-like its dusky panic creeps in the end to your proud
  heart:
O you will feel its kisses cold while it rends your limbs
  apart.
Have you not seen the withering rose and watched the
  lovely moon's decay,
And more than mortal loveliness fade like the fainting
  stars away?

I have seen lovely thoughts forgot in wind, effacing
  dreams;
And dreams like roses wither leaving perfume not nor
  scent;
And I have tried to hold in net like silver fish the sweet
  starbeams,
But all these things are shadowed gleams of things beyond
  the firmament.

EARLIER POEMS

1912

RAPHAEL *

Dear, I have done; it shall be done.   I know
I can paint on and on, and still paint on.
Another touch, and yet another touch.
Yet wherefore?   'Tis Art's triumph to know this,
Long ere the soul and brain begin to flag,
And dim the first fresh flashes of the soul,
Before achievement, by our own desire
And loathing to desist in what we love,
Is wrought to ruin by much overtoil,
To know the very moment of our gain,
And fix the triumph with reluctant pause.
Come from the throne, sweet, kiss me on the cheek;
You have borne bravely, sweet, come, look with me.
Is it not well—think love—the recompense,
This binds the unborn ages at our feet.
Thus you shall look, my love, and never change
Throughout all changes.   Time's own conqueror,
While worshippers of climes and times unknown
Lingeringly look in wonder—here—at us.

What have we done—in these long hours, my love?
Long—long to you—whose patient labour was
To sit, and sit, a statue, movelessly.
Love we have woven a chain more glorious
Than crowns or Popes—to bind the centuries.
You are tired.   I should have thought a little.
But you said nothing, sweet, and I forgot,
In rapture of my soul's imaginings.
You—yes, 'twas thus you looked, ah, look again
That hint of smile—it was like wings for heaven,
And gave my spirit play to revel more
In dazzling visions.   But ah! it mocked my hand.
There—there—before my eyes and in my brain
Limned perfect—but my fingers traitors were.
Could not translate, and heartsick was the strife.

But it is done—I know not how—perchance
Even as I, maddened, drew on hopelessly,
An angel taking pity—mayhap for thee—
Guided my hand and drew it easily.

And they will throng—admire with gaping mouth,
The students, 'Look, what ease, what grace divine.
What balance and what harmony serene'.
And some, 'Like noonday lakes to torrents wild,
After titanic Mighty Angelo'.
Ah, Angelo, he has no sweetness—true.
But, ah, I would I had his breadth of wing.
Jove's Thunders, and the giant craggy heights
Whose points cleave the high heavens, and at
        whose feet
The topmost clouds have end, afraid to soar.

And I too, shake my brow amongst the stars.
And this I know and feel, what I have done
Is but the seed plot of a mightier world.
Yea, world on world is forming in my brain.
I have no space to hold it.   Time will show
I could draw down the Heavens, I could bend
Yon hoar age-scorning column with my hand
I feel such power.   But where there's sun there's
        shade!
And these thoughts bring their shadow in their train.
Who lives?—see this, it is my hand—my name.
But who looks from the canvas, no—not me.
Some doubt of God—but the world lives who
        doubts?
Even thus our own creations mock at us.
Our own creations outlive our decay.

What do I labour for if all is thus?
I triumph, but my triumph is my scorn.

165

'Tis true I love my labour, and the days
Pass pleasantly,
But what is it I love in it—desire
Accomplished?   Never have I reached
The halfway of the purpose I have planned.
A hardship conquered?—a poor juggler's feat
And his elatement mayhap betters mine.
The adoration of the gaping crowd,
Who praise, with jest, not knowing why they
      praise,
Then turn, and sing a lewd and smutty song.
Or kneel—bate breath—to my Lord Cardinal.
Or is it the approval of the wise?
I take it—sadly knowing what I know,
And feeling that this marvel of their world
Is little triumph to me, it being my world.
Their deeds being circumscribed—proportionate,
Within their limits; and mine loftier,
But (God how bounded yet) to do as thus
Is but my nature—therefore little pride
Their praises give me.   Ah, but this gives pride
To know that there is one that does feel pride
When they praise me, and cannot hide the glow
Upon her cheeks to hear me spoken of.
Love—this is better—here—to be with you,
My head upon your bosom while your hair
A loosened fire falls all about my face,
And through its tangles—like a prison bar
To shut my soul in—watch the shadows creep,
The long grey shadows creeping furtively.
I would I were a poet—love—this once.
I cannot tell my feelings. . . .
How effable in this half-light you look,
Love, I would dream—the shadows thickly
      press,
You fade into my fancy—and become
A thought—a smile—a rapture of the brain,

166

A presence that embraces all things felt—
A twilight glamour—faery fantasy.
Your two eyes in the shadow, stars that dream
In quiet waters of the evening, draw
My spirit to them and enfold me there.
Love, I would sleep, dear love I would forget.
Love I would sleep, you watching, covering me,
Charmed by your love and sheltered 'neath love's
        wing,
Sweet, let the world pass as this day has passed,
What do you murmur—sleeping?   Then will I.

KNOWLEDGE   *

Within this glass he looks at he is fair,
Godlike his reach and shining in his eyes
The light that is the sun of Paradise.
Yet midst his golden triumph a despair
Lurks like a serpent hidden in his hair
And says 'Proud wisdom I am yet more wise'.
But swift before his look the serpent dies,
Before his glory's grandeur mirrored there.

This to himself, but what to us looks he?
A lank unresting spectre whose grey gaze,
A moth by night—a ferret through the days—
A hunger that devours all it can see
And then feeds on himself but never slays,
Insatiate with his own misery.

PSYCHE'S LAMENT   *

O! love, my love! once, and not long,
Yet seems it dreams of ancient days,
When nights were passion's lips of song,
And thou his speech of honied praise,
'O love, my love', in murmurs low
Burnt in my ears.   Then I was thine.
O! love, my love! 'twixt weepings now
The empty words are only mine.

O! sweetest love!   O! cruel wings,
The darkening shadow of thy flight
Is all that dreary daylight brings
Of all that was so sweet at night.
O! sweetest love! once you called sweet,
Through kisses, her forlorn who weeps
That wings, too swift to hear their beat,
Of Time, flew with you. . . . How he creeps.

O life, my life!   I have no life
Whilst thou who hast my soul art far.
When night is not, while day has strife,
What life has the unwakened star?
O! life, my life, upon my brow
My tears like flowers are gathered up.
The fruit that sorrow did not sow
She turns to poison in her cup.

'EVEN NOW YOUR EYES ARE MIXED IN MINE' *

Even now your eyes are mixed in mine.
I see you not, but surely, he—
This stricken gaze, has looked on thee.
From him your glances shine.

Even now I felt your hand in mine,
This breeze that warms my open palm
Has surely kist yours; such thrilled calm
No lull can disentwine.

The words you spoke just now, how sweet!
These grasses heard and bend to tell.
The green grows pale your speech to spell,
How its green heart must beat!

I breathe you.   Here the air enfolds
Your absent presence, as fire cleaves,
Leaving the places warm it leaves.
Such warmth a warm word holds.

Bruised are our words and our full thought
Breaks like dull rain from some rich cloud.
Our pulses leap alive and proud.
Colour, not heat, is caught.

AS WE LOOK *

As they have sung to me,
So shall they sing to you?
One song have they.
Nay, when the old be new,
Nay, when the blind shall see,
Then, when the night is day,
Shall this thing be.

For this is truth, and still
Ever throughout be truth
While the world sings.
Gladly it sings to youth;
Sadly to age and ill.
To love sweet whisperings
Its songs fulfil.

One song the roses sing;
One song the chirping birds.
But whoso hears,
He makes within the words
To his soul murmuring.
High hopes or lowly fears
One song shall bring.

One song, one voice, the sky:
The star, the moon, the cloud:
One song the trees.
But some will see a shroud,
And some will dim descry
Immortal harmonies
That never die.

Each looks with eyes that are
But the soul's curtain hung

Till thought draws clear.
One hears sweet songs, un-
    sung
To some, and dumb the star,
To these while songs are near,
Fair things are far.

TWILIGHT   *

[I]

A murmur of many waters, a moving maze of streams;
A doubtful voice of the silence from the ghosts of the
    shadows of dreams,
The far adieu of the day as it touches the fingers of night,
Wakes all to the eye and ear but seem wings spread for
    the soul for flight.

Can we look behind or before us, can we look on the
    dreams that are done?
The lights gleam dim in the distance, the distance is
    dimmer when won.
Soon that shall fade dimmer behind us, and when the
    night before us is here,
Ah! who of us shall wait for the dawn, while the shadows
    of night disappear?

'LIKE SOME FAIR SUBTLE POISON' *

Like some fair subtle poison is the cold white beauty you
    shed;
Pale flower of the garden I walk in, your scent is an
    amorous net
To lure my thoughts and pulses, by your useless phantom
    led
By misty hours and ruins with insatiate longing wet.

To lure my soul with the beauty of some enthralling sin,
To starve my body to hunger for the mystic rapture
    there—
O cruel; flesh and spirit your robe's soft stir sucks in,
And your cold unseeing glances, and the fantasies of your
    hair.

And in the shining hollow of your dream-enhaunted
    throat
My mournful thoughts now wander and build desire a
    nest,
But no tender thoughts to crown the fiery dreams that
    float
Around those sinuous rhythms and dim languors of your
    breast.

LOVE TO BE   *

When at that happy pause that holds sweet rest
As a hard burden, that it doth belate
And make him seem a laggard at the gate
Of long-wished night, while day rides down the
        west;
I, weighted from my toil, and sore distrest
In body and soul, the scourge of partial fate,
At such sweet pause, to silence consecrate,
Came thoughts swift changing fancy had bedrest
In colours of desire.   I thought on her
I never yet have seen, my love to be.
I conjured up all glorious shapes that were;
And wondered what far clime, by what sad sea
She roaming?   And what spirits minister?
What thoughts, and what vague shadowing of
        me?

By what far ways shall my heart reach to thine?
We, who have never parted—never met,
Nor done to death the joys that shall be yet,
Nor drained the cup of love's delirious wine.
How shall my craving spirit know for mine
Thine, self-same seeking?   Will a wild regret
For the lost days—the lonely suns that set,
Be for our love a token and a sign?
Will all the weary nights, the widowed days
That sundered long, all point their hands at
        thee?
Yea! all the stars that have not heard thy praise
Low murmur in thy charmèd ear of me?
All pointing to the ending of the ways,
All singing of the love that is to be?

YOU AND I *

You and I have met but for an instant;
And no word the gate-lips let from out them.
But the eyes, voice audible—the soul's lips,
Stirr'd the depths of thought and feeling in me.

I have seen you somewhere, some sweet sometime,
Somewhere in a dim-remembered sometime.
Was it in the sleep-spun realm of dreamland?
In sweet woods, a faery flower of fancy?

If our hands touched would it bring us nearer?
As our souls touched, eyes' flame meeting eyes'
        flame.
If the lips spake would it lift the curtain
More than our mute bearing unaffected
Told the spirit's secrets eloquently?

Strange! this vast and universal riddle!
How perplexing!   Manifold the wonder.
You and I, we meet but for an instant,
Pause or pass, reflections in a mirror.
And I see myself and wonder at it.
See myself in you, a double wonder.
With my thought held in a richer casket,
Clothed and girt in shape of regal beauty.
Strange! we pause!   New waves of life rush
        blindly,
Madly on the soul's dumb silent breakers.

And a music strange is new awakened.
Fate the minstrel smites or holds the chord back.
Smites—new worlds undreamt of burst upon us.
All our life before was but embryo
Shaping for this birth—this living moment.

* ©   174

DON JUAN'S SONG

The moon is in an ecstasy,
It wanes not nor can grow.
The heavens are in a mist of
    love,
And deepest knowledge know.
What things in nature seem to
    move
Bear love as I bear love?
And bear my pleasures so?

The moon will fade when morn-
    ing comes,
The heavens will dream no more
In our missed meetings are eyes
    hard?
What shadows fleck the door
Averted, when we part?   What
    guard
Scents death in each vain word?
What haggard haunts the shore?

I bear my love as streams that
    bear
The sky still flow or shake—
Though deep within too far on
    high.
Light blossoms kiss and wake
The waters sooner than the sky.
And if they kiss and die!
God made them frail to break.

MY SONGS *

Deep into the great heart of things
My mood passed, as my life became
One with the vasty whisperings
That breathe the pure ineffable name.

A pulse of all the life that stirs
Through still deep shade and waver-
    ing light,
The flowing of the wash of years
From out the starry infinite.

And flowing through my soul the
    skies
And all the winds and all the trees
Mixed with its stream of light, to
    rise
And flow out in these melodies.

TO NATURE *

Beneath the eternal wandering
    skies
O wilt thou rest awhile by me,
Immortal mother of mystery,
And breathe on my blind eyes!

Or is it that thou standest nigh,
And while I know that I am blind
I live, until thou passest by,
To leave me dead behind.

                1912

THE POET *

[I]

The trouble of the universe is on his wonder-travelled
    eyes.
Ah, vain for him the starry quest, the spirit's wistful
    sacrifice.
For though the glory of the heavens celestially in
    glimpses seen
Illumines his rapt gazing, still the senses shut him in.
No fellowship of suffering to meet his tear-bewildered
    ways,
Alone he bears the burden of alienated days.
He is a part of paradise that all the earth has pressed
    between,
And when he calls unto the stars of paradise with heaven-
    sweet songs
To his divided self he calls and sings the story of earth's
    wrongs.

Himself he has himself betrayed, and deemed the earth a
    path of heaven,
And wandered down its sunless days, and too late knew
    himself bereaven.
For swiftly sin and suffering and earth-born laughter
    meshed his ways,
And caught him in a cage of earth, but heaven can hear his
    dewy lays.

1912

'O'ER THE CELESTIAL PATHWAYS' *

O'er the celestial pathways the mortal and immortal
    strays;
For earth is a swift dream of God, and man one shape
    within His brain.
And there man meeteth sun and moon, immortal shapes
    of nights and days,
And in God's glad mood he is glad and in God's petu-
    lance has pain.

And there he dreams his dreamer's face; forgets, nor
    knows himself a dream,
Until some shadow wavers by and leaves him but a
    trembling shade
To murmur in his impotence that nothing is, but all
    things seem,
And what they seem like man shall know when man
    beneath the dust is laid.

1912

FLEET STREET *

From north and south, from east and
  west,
Here in one shrieking vortex meet
These streams of life, made manifest
Along the shaking quivering street.
Its pulse and heart that throbs and glows
As if its strife were its repose.

I shut my ear to such rude sounds
As reach a harsh discordant note,
Till, melting into what surrounds,
My soul doth with the current float,
And from the turmoil and the strife
Wakes all the melody of life.

The stony buildings blindly stare
Unconscious of the crime within,
While man returns his fellow's glare
The secrets of his soul to win.
And each man passes from his place,
None heed. A shadow leaves such
  trace.

'WE ARE SAD WITH A VAGUE SWEET SORROW' *

We are sad with a vague sweet sorrow
Whose touch is a scent of sighs;
A flower that weeps to a flower
The old tale that beauty dies.

Our smiles are full of a longing,
For we saw the gold flash of the years.
They passed, and we know where they
        came from,
The deep—deep well of tears.

1912

PEACE   *

Where the dreamy mountains brood
Ever in their ancient mood
Would I go and dream with them
Till I graft me on their stem.

With fierce energy I aspire
To be that the Gods desire
As the dreamy mountains are
And no God can break or mar.

Soon the world shall fade and be
One with still eternity
As the dreamy hills that lie
Silent to the passing sky.

1912

So innocent you spread your net,
I knew not I was caught in it,
Till when I vainly tried to rise
I read the reason in your eyes.

Your silken smiles had bound me
      fast;
Your nestling speech had tangled
      more;
But when I started up at last
I shook the fetters to the floor.

THE NUN

So thy soul's meekness shrinks,
Too loth to show her face—
Why should she shun the world?
It is a holy place.

Concealèd to itself
If the flower kept its scent,
Of itself amorous,
Less rich its ornament.

Use—utmost in each kind—
Is beauty, truth in one,
While soul rays light to soul
In one God-linkèd sun.

Now the spirit's song has
    withered
As a song of last year's June
That has made the air its tomb.
Shall we ever find it after
Sighing in some summer tune
That is sealèd now in gloom,
Safe for light and laughter?

Now the sky.blooms full of
    colour,
Houses glow and windows shine
Glittering with impatient
    wings.
Where they go to may I follow
Since mine eyes have made them
    mine?
Shall I ever find these things
Hid in hill or hollow?

BACCHANAL   *

If life would come to me
As she has never come,
The music of the spring,
The fullness of its prime;
With roses in her hair,
With laughter on her lips,
Ah! life!—we'd dance a tune.
Ah! life! we'd live—we'd live.

If life would come to me
With roses in her lap,
With wine between her hands,
And a fire upon her lips;
We would burn Time in that fire,
We would drown care in that wine,
And with music and with laughter
We would scare black death away.

If life would only come
As I would have her come,
With sweet breasts for my bed,
And my food her fiery wine;
If life would only come,
For we live not till it comes,
And it comes not till we feel
Its fire through all our veins.

THE CAGE *

Air knows as you know that I sing in my cage of earth,
And my mouth dry with longing for your winsome
    mouth of mirth,
That passes ever my prison bars which will not fall apart,
Wearied unweariedly so long with the fretful music of
    my heart.

If you were a rose, and I, the wandering invisible air
To feed your scent and live, glad though you knew me
    not there,
Or the green of your stem that your proud petals could
    never meet,
I yet would feel the caresses of your shadow's ruby feet.

O splendour of radiant flesh, O your heavy hair uncurled,
Binding all that my hopes have fashioned to crown me
    King of the world,
I sing to life to befriend me; she sends me your mouth
    of mirth,
And you only laugh as you pass me, and I weep in my
    cage of earth.

THE KEY OF THE GATES OF HEAVEN *

A word leapt sharp from my tongue,
Could a golden key do more
Than open the golden door
For the rush of the golden song?
She spoke, and the spell of her speech—
The chain of the heart linked song—
Was on me swift and strong,
And Heaven was in my reach.

A word was the key thereof;
And my thought was the hand that turned.
And words that throbbed and burned,
Sweet birds from the shine of love,
Flew clear 'tween the rosebud gate
That was parted beneath and above,
And a chain of music wove
More strong than the hand of fate.

NOCTURNE *

Day, like a flower of gold fades on its crimson bed;
For the many chambered night unbars to shut its sweet-
    ness up;
From earth and heaven fast drawn together a heavy still-
    ness is shed,
And our hearts drink the shadowy splendour from a
    brimming cup.

For the indrawn breath of beauty thrills the holy caves of
    night;
Shimmering winds of heaven fall gently and mysterious
    hands caress
Our wan brows with cooling rapture of the delicate star-
    light
Dropping from the night's blue walls in endless veils of
    loveliness.

THE PRESENT *

Time, leveller, chaining fate itself to thee—
Hope frets her eager pettings on thy sand,
Wild waves that strive to overreach command
Of nature, much in sight.   Eternity
Is but thyself made shoreless.   Toward thy sea
The streams-to-be flow from the shadowland
Of rootless flowers no earthly breeze has fanned,
Weave with the past thy restless apathy.

Thou art the link 'twixt after and before,
The one sole truth; the final ultimate
Endeavour of the ages.   The loud roar
Of life around me is thy voice to fate
And Time—who looking on thee has grown hoar
While thou art yet—and freedom is so late.

BIRTHDAY SONG *

To thy cradle at thy birth
Did not all the fairies come,
Genie of heaven and earth
While ogres stood afar and dumb,

And thy cradle to embower
Spun a roof of sun and flowers,
Gave thee for thy lifelong dower
Beauteous gifts and beauteous hours?

Time stood by, a gardener mild,
Watched the bud unfold to rose,
June's delight December's child,
Red rose of December snows.

Twenty years and one year more
Time here layeth at thy feet;
But thy friends bring twenty score
Wishes that the rest be sweet.

* ©

EARLIER POEMS
BEFORE 1912

'GOD LOOKED CLEAR AT ME THROUGH HER EYES' *

God looked clear at me through her
    eyes,
And when her fresh and sweet lips
    spake,
Through dawn-flushed gates of
    Paradise
Such silvern birds did wing and shake

God's fervent music on my soul,
And with their jewelled quivering feet
Did rend apart the quiet stole
That shades from girl-fanned pulsing
    heat.

Upon a gold branch in my breast
They made their nest, while sweet
    and warm
Hung wav'ring thoughts like rose-
    leaves drest;
My soul the sky to keep from harm.

In the heart's woods mysterious
Where feelings lie remote and far,
They fly with touch imperious,
And loose emotion's hidden bar.

And to dark pools of brooding care,
And blinding wastes of loneliness,
They gleam a Paradisal air,
And warm with a divine caress.

LINES WRITTEN IN AN ALBUM *

The birds that sang in summer
Were silent till the spring;
For hidden were the flowers,
The flowers to whom they sing.
December's jewelled bosom—
Closed mouth—hill-hidden vale—
Held seed full soon to blossom:
Held song that would not fail.

I, silent all the winter,
No flower for me to praise,
For this rich wealth of roses
My song shall I not raise?
The lilies and the roses,
White hands and damask cheeks;
The eyes where love reposes
And laughs before he speaks.

Could this make music to thee,
The music of sweet thought;
Thy laughing eyes might hearken
To sounds sweet visions wrought,
Till the deep roses tingle
The cheeks they nestle in,
While music still would mingle,
And pleasure still begin.

Thus, hidden in these pages,
My thoughts shall silent lie
Till gentle fingers find them
When idly bent to pry.
I see them fondly linger,
And quicken with their breath
The music of the singer,
Whose silence was its death.

TO MR. AND MRS. LOWY, ON THEIR SILVER WEDDING *

'Ye hearken as ye list', saith Time to all.
'Ye hear me as I pass or do not hear.
I gather all the fruits of all the year,
I hoard them when the barren seasons call.
Then, though I flew with Spring, with
    them I crawl.
To soothe their vacant eyes and feet of fear
I bid the Spring's sweet ghost rise from
    her bier,
And tender Memory come with light foot-
    fall.

'Then, when the seasons hang their heads in
    shame
And grief, I bring my store of hoarded fruit;
To warm the hands of age, youth's rosy
    flame;
And to old love the young love at the root,
Hallowed by me to silver sweet acclaim—
Hush—lo! the bride and bridegroom—
    hush!—be mute.'

1911

'THE WORLD RUMBLES BY ME' *

The world rumbles by me—can I heed?
The rose it is crimson—and I bleed.

The rose of my heart glows deep afar;
And I grope in the darkness 'twixt star
    and star.

Only in night grows the flower of peace,
Spreading its odours of rest and ease.

It dies in the day like light in the night.
It revives like tears in the eyes of delight.

For the youth at my heart beats wild and
    loud;
And raves in my ear of a girl and a shroud.

Of a golden girl with the soul in her eyes,
To teach me love and to make me wise.

With the fire on her lips and the wine in her
    hands,
To bind me strong in her silken bands.

For time and fate are striding to meet
One unseen with soundless feet.

The world rustles by me—let me heed.
Clutched in its madness till I bleed.

For the rose of my heart glows deep afar.
If I stretch my hand, I may clasp a star.

MY DAYS

My days are but the tombs of buried hours;
Which tombs are hidden in the pilèd years;
But from the mounds there springeth up such
    flowers
Whose beauty well repays its cost of tears.
Time, like a sexton, pileth mould on mould,
Minutes on minutes till the tombs are high;
But from the dust there falleth grains of gold,
And the dead corpse leaves what will never die.
It may be but a thought, the nursling seed
Of many thoughts, of many a high desire;
Some little act that stirs a noble deed,
Like breath rekindling a smouldering fire.
They only live who have not lived in vain,
For in their works their life returns again.

In the heart of the forest,
The shuddering forest,
The moaning and sobbing
Sad shuddering forest—
The dark and the dismal
Persistent sad sobbing
Throughout the weird forest.

Ah! God! they are voices—
Dim ghosts of the forest
Unrestfully sobbing
Through wistful pale voices,
Whose breath is the wind and whose
    lips the sad trees;

Whose yearning great eyes
Death haunted for ever
Look from the dark waters,
And pale spirit faces
Wrought from the white lilies.

This was meant for an album.   [*Author's note in MS.*]

THE DEAD PAST   *

Ah! will I meet you ever—you who have gone from
    me,
You, the I that was then and a moment hath changed
    into you.
So many moments have passed and changed the I into
    we,
So many many times but alas I remember so few.

I know you are dead, long perished, the boy that babbled
    and played
With the toys like the wind with the flowers and the
    clouds play with the moon,
I know you are dead long ago and hid in the grave I
    made
Of regrets that were soon forgotten, as snow is forgotten
    by June.

You too are dead, the shining face that laughed and wept
    without thought
Uttered the words of the heart, wept or leapt as was right.
O, were you taken to heaven, by God in a whirlwind
    caught,
I do not know yours was best, you not conscious of your
    delight.

O my life's dead Springtime—why will you haunt me like
    ghosts,
You little buds that have died—and blossom in memory,
Will I meet you in some dead land and see your faces in
    hosts,
Saying 'The past is the future and you and the future are
    we'?

DEATH *

Death waits for me—ah! who shall kiss me first?
No lips of love glow red from out the gloom
That life spreads darkly like a living tomb
Around my path.   Death's gift is best, not worst.
For even the honey on life's lips is curst.
And the worm cankers in the ripest bloom.
Yea, from Birth's gates to Death's, Life's travailed
   womb
Is big with Rest, for Death, her life, athirst.

Death waits, and when she has kissed Life's warm
   lips
With her pale mouth, and made him one with her;
Held to him Lethe's wine whereof he sips;
And stilled Time's wings, earth-shadowing sleepless
   whir;
Outside of strife, beyond the world's blood-drips,
Shadowed by peace, Rest dwells and makes no stir.

                                        1910

197

A BALLAD OF TIME, LIFE AND MEMORY *

Hold wide the door and watch who passes here
From dawn through day to dawn,
Bravely as though their journey but begun,
Through change unchangèd still.
She, wild-eyed, runs and laughs, or walks and
    weeps;
But him, swift-footed, never can outrun,
Nor creep and he before.
And all she has and all she knows is his;
But not all his for her.

He gives her of the spices and the myrrh
And wonderful strange fruits,
He gives her more of tears, and girds her round
With yearning bitterness,
With fears that kill the hopes they feed upon,
With hopes that smile at fears and smile on her,
Till fears again prevail.
And as she goes the roses fall and die;
And as she goes she weeps.

But lo! behind, what dim processional?
What maiden sings and sighs?
And holds an urn, and as the roses fall,
And the wine pours and spills,
She gathers in her lap and breathes on them;
And in the urn the spilled wine glows again,
Lit by her eyes divine.
And all the roses at her touch revive,
And blush and bloom again.

And by her side, whose name is Memory,
The ghosts of all the hours,

Some smiling as they smiled within the sun,
Some, stained and wan with tears.
To those she gives the roses as they fall,
And bids them tune the praises of their prime.
To these their tears and dust.
And those are happy loves and wreathèd joys.
And these are sorrows pale.

Even as she sings so Time himself makes pause,
Even Time, Death's conqueror,
And Life's reverted face grows tenderer,
While the soul dreams and yearns,
Watching the risen faces of the hours,
And shrivelled autumn change her face to June's,
And dead wine live again,
And dust discrowned know Life it knew before
Touched with a softened light.

There is no leaf upon the naked woods,
No bird upon the boughs,
And Time leads Life through many waste places,
And dreams and shapes of death.
Yet is the voice of Summer not quite dumb,
Although her lips be stilled and silenter.
For Memory bids her rise
To sing within the palace of the soul,
And Life and Time are still.

1910

A BALLAD OF WHITECHAPEL

God's mercy shines,
And our full hearts must make record of this,
For grief that burst from out its dark confines
Into strange sunlit bliss.

I stood where glowed
The merry glare of golden whirring lights
Above the monstrous mass that seethed and
　　　flowed
Through one of London's nights.

I watched the gleams
Of jaggèd warm lights on shrunk faces pale.
I heard mad laughter as one hears in dreams,
Or Hell's harsh lurid tale.

The traffic rolled,
A gliding chaos populous of din.
A steaming wail at doom the Lord had
　　　scrawled
For perilous loads of sin.

And my soul thought,
'What fearful land have my steps wandered
　　　to?
God's love is everywhere, but here is naught
Save love His anger slew.'

And as I stood
Lost in promiscuous bewilderment,
Which to my mazèd soul was wonder-food,
A girl in garments rent

Peered 'neath lids shamed,
And spoke to me and murmured to my
	blood.
My soul stopped dead, and all my horror
	flamed
At her forgot of God.

Her hungered eyes,
Craving and yet so sadly spiritual,
Shone like the unsmirched corner of a jewel
Where else foul blemish lies.

I walked with her
Because my heart thought, 'Here the soul is
	clean,
The fragrance of the frankincense and myrrh
Is lost in odours mean.'

She told me how
The shadow of black death had newly come
And touched her father, mother, even now
Grim-hovering in her home,

Where fevered lay
Her wasting brother in a cold bleak room,
Which theirs would be no longer than a day—
And then—the streets and doom.

Lord! Lord! dear Lord!
I knew that life was bitter, but my soul
Recoiled, as anguish-smitten by sharp sword,
Grieving such body's dole.

Then grief gave place
To a strange pulsing rapture as she spoke,
For I could catch the glimpses of God's
    grace,
And a desire awoke

To take this trust,
And warm and gladden it with love's new
    fires,
Burning the past to ashes and to dust
Through purified desires.

We walked our way,
One way hewn for us from the birth of Time.
For we had wandered into Love's strange
    clime
Through ways sin waits to slay.

Love's euphony,
In Love's own temple that is our glad hearts,
Makes now long music wild deliciously,
Now Grief hath used his darts.

Love infinite,
Chastened by sorrow, hallowed by pure
    flame—
Not all the surging world can compass it.
Love—love—O! tremulous name.

God's mercy shines.
And my full heart hath made record of this,
Of grief that burst from out its dark confines
Into strange sunlit bliss.

DAWN BEHIND NIGHT *

Lips! bold, frenzied utterance, shape to the thoughts that
    are prompted by hate
Of the red streaming burden of wrong we have borne and
    still bear;
That wealth with its soul-crushing scourges placed into its
    hands by fate,
Hath made the cement of its towers, grim-girdled by our
    despair.

Should it die in the death that they make, in the silence
    that follows the sob;
In the voiceless depth of the waters that closes upon our
    grief;
Who shall know of the bleakness assigned us for the fruits
    that we reap and they rob?—
To pour out the strong wine of pity, outstretch the kind
    hand in relief.

In the golden glare of the morning, in the solemn serene
    of the night,
We look on each other's faces, and we turn to our prison
    bar;
In pitiless travail of toil and outside the precious light,
What wonder we know not our manhood in the curse of
    the things that are?

In the life or the death they dole us from the rags and the
    bones of their store,
In the blood they feed but to drink of, in the pity they
    feign in their pride,
Lies the glimpse of a heaven behind it, for the ship hath
    left the shore,
That will find us and free us and take us where its portals
    are opened wide.

1909

ZION

She stood—a hill-ensceptred Queen,
　　The glory streaming from her;
While Heaven flashed her rays between,
　　And shed eternal summer.

The gates of morning opened wide
　　On sunny dome and steeple.
Noon gleamed upon the mountain-side
　　Throng'd with a happy people.

And twilight's drowsy, half closed eyes
　　Beheld that virgin splendour
Whose orbs were as her darkening skies,
　　And as her spirit, tender.

Girt with that strength, first-born of right,
　　Held fast by deeds of honour,
Her robe she wove with rays more bright
　　Than Heaven could rain upon her.

Where is that light—that citadel?
　　That robe with woof of glory?
She lost her virtue and she fell,
　　And only left her story.

1906

ODE TO DAVID'S HARP *

Awake, ye joyful strains! awake,
In silence sleep no more;
Disperse the gloom that ever lies
O'er Judah's barren shore.
Where are the hands that strung thee
With tender touch and true?
Those hands are silenced, too.

The harp that faster caused to beat
The heart that throbbed for war,
The harp that melancholy calmed,
Lies mute on Judah's shore.
One chord awake—one strain prolong
To wake the zeal in Israel's breast;
Oh sacred lyre, once more, how long?
'Tis vain, alas! in silence rest.

Many a minstrel fame's elated
Envies thee thy harp of fame,
Harp of David—monarch minstrel,
Bravely—bravely, keep thy name.
Ay! ev'ry ear that listen'd,
Was charmed—was thrilled—was
        bound.
Every eye with moisture glisten'd
Thrilling to the harp's sweet sound.

Hark! the harp is pouring
Notes of burning fire,
And each soul o'erpowering,
Melts the rousing ire.
Fiercer—shriller—wilder far
Than the iron notes of war,
Accents sweet and echoes sweeter,
Minstrel—minstrel, steeds fly fleeter
Spurred on by thy magic strains.

Tell me not the harp lies sleeping,
Set not thus my heart aweeping,
In the muse's fairy dwelling
There thy magic notes are swelling.
But for list'ning mortals' ear
Vainly wait, ye will not hear.
So clearly sweet—so plaintive sad
More tender tone no harper had.
O! when again shall Israel see
A harp so toned with melody?

1905

FRAGMENTS   *

ADAM

[*The following is a fragment of a play called 'Adam',
or 'Adam and Lilith', which Rosenberg abandoned in
favour of 'The Unicorn'. Chronologically it came
just before the latter play, and it includes a theme that
reappears in parts of that; it is, however, too distinct
in conception to be placed among the other fragments
of 'The Unicorn'.*]

SPIRIT OF DISSOLUTION.   LILITH

SPIRIT. Crazed shadow from your golden body
    Lilith, Lilith, I am.
    I am a tremor in space
    Caught in your beauty's grasp.
    My tentacles that bore so secretly
    Into the health of the world, go suddenly lax.
    When my pulses pale to your beauty's music
    At night in your bed chamber
    Cruel your glimmering mirror shakes,
    As my thoughts, my pulses, pass
    Hungry to you, to roam your vivid beauty.
    Do you not hear their moan
    Beside those four lips darkened in glee,
    Shapeless in voluntary glee,
    Two where mine should be
    Of his your master Adam,
    Whose common bread you are
    Now he is hungry no more?
    Lilith—be kind.
LILITH. If you are stronger than Adam.
SPIRIT. For your sake only, girl,
    I have been cruel to my instinct
    And the venom in my hand.
    For your sake, and the mutable winds of love.

LILITH. I am beautiful.
SPIRIT. Ask Adam.
LILITH. He is a widower since I died to him.
SPIRIT. I am a ghost and you are, we will wed then.
LILITH. I was a lover without a lover.
SPIRIT. Let him be king without a kingdom,
  Let me destroy a city, his people.

II

[*The following poem was written for a Christmas
card that Rosenberg drew for his Division in* 1917.]

British women! in your wombs you plotted
This monstrous girth of glory, this marvel-
    lous glory.
Not for mere love-delights God meant the
    profound hour
When an Englishman was planned.
Responsible hour! wherein God wrote anew
His guarantee of the world's surety
Of honour, light and sweetness, all forgot
Since men first marred the writ of Mary's
    Son.

III

Learn not such music here.
The grave's door
Shall hear that music
Of the Eternal taciturn.

[This was sent in a letter, with the note: 'The other side is doggerel I've just written'.]

TO WILHELM II

It is cruel Emperor
The stars are too high.
For your reach Emperor
Far out they lie.
It is cruel for you Emperor
The sea has a stone,
England—they call it Eng-
    land,
That cannot shine in your
    crown.

Cruel the seas are deep,
Cruel for you Emperor
That all men are not in blind
    sleep,
And free hearts burn, Emperor.
It is cruel when a wronged
    world turns
And draws the claws of the
    beast
Cruel, cruel for you Emperor
Who would be most is least.

[*Fragment from an earlier conception of 'Moses'.*]

MOSES. I feel inert, strange, a losing of myself,
    A presence as though million years were forcing
    Into me.
    I will light a fire.
        [*The angel appears out of the burning bush*]
MOSES. I see no shape.   I look for my own soul.
    Your fold is not a butchery.   Run, dog,
    I cannot bring the fold here—make them frisk.
    Why do they cower so,
    Huddled and bleating?
    Vivid on their brains the tawny panther races.
    Nothing. . . . What can they mean?
    Yesterday's same nibbled slopes,
    The same sun's key to open same safe miles.
    O, woolly white flocks,
    I will allow your anguished self-conceit
    And knowledge of your unique purpose here
    To line man's belly inside and without,
    But what should stir it now?
    What secret terror, what instinct doth
    Coax the safe hill to frighted meanings, and
    Give such earnest cunning praises
    To life by that deep terror?

Power that impels,
Pulse of the void working to my vain grap-
    pling fingers,
Like a grave star drawing our gazes forlorn
Will kiss the sister star that is my soul,
So I a visible star, would penetrate the vast,
The unimaginable chasms and abysses
To reach the fountain star that hides the soul
    of thee.

The poet's dead soul whose flung word lights
    the world,
The struck music that panic whirls the world—
The hills decay and pass to blossoms of fire;
In their slow dust God kneads his changing
    forms.
Sculptor of infinite dreams, we thank our
    dreamer.

VII
EVENING

My roses loiter, lips to press
Of emerald winds
Fall'n from sky chasms of sunset stress. . . .
Amongst their petals grope
Displacing hands, and vapoured heliotrope.

The vague viols of evening
Call all the flower clans
To some abysmal swinging
And tumult of deep trance.

1915

VIII

ART

O amber anger thrust
Out of a madman's lust
For a balked perfection,
Sad lithe towering—
Eternal dereliction.

Barbaric tenderness
Burns swart for sorrowless
Roses in storm adance,
Abysmal as thy swing
Through a tumult of deep trance.

IX

[*Another version*]

This maenad anger thrust
Out of a madman's lust
For a balked perfection,
This lithe towering
Of life to dereliction.

Barbaric tenderness
Swart and blithe as the stress
Of storm on rose adance,
Abysmal to swing
In your tumult of trance.

The riding pomp of the years,
Vigorous our eyes and ears
When from your arm
Silence is flung, from a sling
To sound song's alarm.

The streaming vigours of our blood
Where silence is a derelict;
Life's derelict, poesy,
Saith Life's no derelict of hers.
The riding pomp of all the years
Her sinews are and bone, saith she.

X

Ah, if your lips might stir,
With one mood's breath behind,
To the touch of a certain mood
As easily as it alters
To all swift moods but this!
But you are afraid to smile
And bewitch yourself to a place
Where though your moods might alter
One mood would come in vain.

XI

There are sweet chains that bind
And gains that are strange loss.
Your ruddy freedom falters
And pales at hint of these.
You change, bewilder and gleam
In a labyrinth of light,
But one change calls dark and dumbly
To you and calls in vain.

1914–1915

XII

You gave me leave to love you—
In my own way I will.
Your leave you gave in your way.

In shy delight of loving,
The ways we two had met
Those ways we still must wander—
There is one thing to forget.

We must forget ourselves, sweet,
Too much we feel the kiss,
Forget the bliss of loving,
And strive for God love's bliss.

1914

XIII

In half delight of shy delight,
In a sweetness thrilled with fears,
Her eyes on the rich storied night,
Reads love and strangely hears
Love guests with wintered years.

We know the summer-plaited hours,
O maiden still plaiting
Your men-unruffled curls
For fierce loving and hating—

1914

XIV

Frail hours that love to dance
To hear yon princely sun,
His golden countenance
Scatters you pale and wan,
Scatters your ghostly love
That was the breath of a dream,
Scatters light from above
Till day flows like a stream.

The stars fade in the sky
Taking our dreams away,
Day's banners flame on high
In gaudy disarray.

1914–1915

XV

But I am thrown with beauty's breath
Climbing my soul, driven in
Like a music wherein is pressed
All the power that withers the mountain
And maketh trees to grow.

From the neck of a God your hands are odorous.
Now I am made a God and he without you is none.
Your eyes still wear the looks of Paradise.
I look upon its shining fields and mourn for the
    outcast angels
Who have no Eden now since it shines in your eyes.

.   .   .   .   .

My soul is a molten cup with brimming music of
    your mouth;
Somewhere is a weeping silence and I feel a
    happy thief.

1914

XVI

A woman's beauty is a strong tree's roots.
The tree is space, its branches hidden lutes,
Wherefrom such music spreads into the air
That all it breathes on doth its spirit share,
And all men's souls are drawn beneath and lie
Mixed into her as words mix with the sky.
And as some words before they mix are stayed
And old thoughts live new spirits by their aid,
So souls of some men meet the spirit of love
That sentinels.

A woman's beauty is like kisses shed,
A colour heard, or thoughts that have been
    said.
It covers, with infinity between.
The memory sees, but 'twixt you and that
    seen
A million ages lie.   It is a wave
That in old time swept Gods, and did enslave
As the broad sea imprisons, savage lands.
It is a wind that blows from careful hands
The grains of gathered wheat, and golden
    grains
To others bears.

It is a diver into seas more strange
Than fishes know.   No poison makes such
    change
As her swift subtle alchemy.

XVII

Amber eyes with ever such little red fires,
Face as vague and white as a swan in shadow.

1914–1915

XVIII

My desires are as the sea
Whose white tongues fawn on the
      breast
Of sand and turn it again to sea,
Back to itself that prest.
My desires feed on me.

XIX

Where the rock's heart is hidden from the sea
The unwearied sea whose white tongues fawn upon
    its breast
The rock's heart hidden from the unwearying sea

Whose white tongues fawn upon its dumb $\begin{cases} \text{wet cheeks} \\ \text{cold breasts} \\ \text{cold cheeks} \end{cases}$

It knows the hunger
O as the rock's heart is her heart
And my thoughts fawn and my eyes cover her
O wonderful sea—it is little rock

Her eyes, $\begin{cases} \text{that are the heavens} \\ \text{deep heavens} \end{cases}$ whose depths reach
                               not to me.

1914

XX

He was mad,
Brain drenched by luxury of pulsing blood,
While to his heart's throat his cold spirit pressed.
And ever rippled waves of golden curls,
Rose hue made of his thoughts a coloured fire.

1914

XXI

The trees suffer the wind,
And the sunbeams leap on their mail.
The shadows slide from leaf to leaf,
And, sudden and brief,
Resounds like an avalanche
The throats of these things frail.

1914

XXII

Heart, is there hope—or is there ordeal still
    in thy stars' horoscope?
Come, the keen years, the fierce years,
    laughing and cruel,
Heap on your trouble.

1914

XXIII

The brooding stones and the dissolving hills,
The summer's leafy luxury,
The winter shrewd,
And all thy changing robes, thy myriad forms.

XXIV

The monster wind prowls in the writhen trees,
The wind dives in the writhen trees,
They strain in angered leash their green,
They are only strong in ease.

Soft, forward, inarticulate,
Warm, wayward, drooping, or aburst,
Rushing, it tires, slacks to abate.

The wind wakes in the writhen trees

1914

XXV

In a concentrated thought a sudden
        noise startles.
Sensual motions of nerves
Vibrate from hushed sky curves,
Helpless, obscene and cruel.
My fires must drain that jewel
Of all its virgin rays.
Crunched in one black amaze
My life inert goes out,
Dissolves voluptuously.

XXVI

O spear-girt face too far
Save for the sorcery that makes soft
Those points or turns them inward on herself.
I cannot cleave through that inviolate tract
That virginal

XXVII

Love, hide thy face—why in thy land
This garden blooms we understand
A little—not at all—but men
Live not who are not drunk sometime
With power of its scents that climb
Their towers of soul and melt and sting,
The thoughted throng unburnishing,
The spiritual shining

Rapid the flames and swords, the chains
Flash and are flung, we burn, we writhe,
The blood is emptied from our veins
And wine streams through, fiercely and blithe,
The royal flesh whose panting legions

1914

XXVIII

Poets have snared you in sweet word;
Such cage, immortal singing bird,
Each soul finds you while tread your eyes
Its intricate infinities,
Bounding infinity in a mood
Whose habit is your roseate hood,
To ecstasy—to ecstasy
More sweet than Paradise can be,
Where every thought and pulse and vein
Melts into joy—till sense is fain
To cease lest

XXIX

Her grape green eyes have stained in weird
Lustrous fantasies the urn
Of one mood and ever they burn,
And the heart stands there to learn.

They are old carvings so long heard
In oldest struggle of man's brain
One of restlessness to gain,
Death dim—fair hair in vain.

XXX

Pale mother night, suckling thy brood of stars,
My fire, too, yearns for thy giant love,
But they are calm, and mine is frenzy fire.

XXXI

In all Love's heady valour and bold pains
Is the wide storehouse for your female gains

XXXII

A flea whose body shone like bead
Gave me delight as I gave heed.

A spider whose legs like stiff thread
Made me think quaintly as I read.

A rat whose droll shape would dart and flit
Was like a torch to light my wit.

A fool whose narrow forehead hung
A wooden target for my tongue.

A meagre wretch in whose generous scum
Himself was lost—his $\begin{Bmatrix} \text{dirty} \\ \text{living} \end{Bmatrix}$ tomb.

But the flea crawled too near—
His blood the smattered wall doth smear

And the spider being too brave
No doctor now can him save.

And when the rat would rape my cheese
He signed the end of his life's lease.

O cockney who maketh negatives,
You negative of negatives.

1914

223

XXXIII

SENSUAL

Or where absence, silence is,
Of fleshly strings whose strains are Paradise
And pavin ecstasies
For the untravelled ardours leashed in eyes.

Youth's fearless wings are spread.
O Cynic life! fine mirrors are your walls.
O voice and lip unwed,
Hands beckon but my own wild shadow calls.

Is not love loveliness,
Truth beauty and all natural harmony
Unstriving happiness,
The mystic centre of all unity?

Life mirrors love and truth
Even as our love and truth within be deep.
His own self dazzles youth

1914

XXXIV

Beautiful is the day,
Sighs the beloved night
Why do you fly away
When I come with my stars bright?
Your gaudy disarray

1914

XXXV

Wood and forest, drink
Of the blue delight,
Only of its brink.
But to my mind and sight
Drink from brink to brink.

XXXVI

I know all men are withered with yearning—
O forest flame, guarded with swords that are
        burning,
O eyes that sea-like our madness entombs,
Gold hair whose rich metal enlocks us in terror

XXXVII

Green thoughts are
Ice block on a barrow
Gleaming in July.
A little boy with bare feet
And jewels at his nose stands by.

XXXVIII

I have heard the Gods
In their high conference
As I lay outside the world
Quiet in sleep

XXXIX

In the large manner and luxury
Of a giant who guests
In a little world of mortals,
He condescends a space
His ears to incline,
But as though list'ning were a trouble.
Who knows! but it were a hazard
To break speech on this matter,
To bid conference with a doctor!
Mayhap cod-liver-oil,
Thrice in the day taken,
Medicinal might be

XL

Even as a letter burns and curls
And the mind and heart in the writing
    blackens,
Words that wane as the wind unfurls—
Obliteration never slackens.
Fate who wrote it and addressed it here,
Life who read it, loved it, called it dear,
Peace who slumbered, Love who tore it
    through.

XLI

The thronging glories ringing round our
    birth,
The angels worshipping, th' adoring kings,
The inspired presence,
Surely the songs, the worship, and the
    burden
Of light washes beneath the lidded slumber
Of the shut soul.

                     1914

XLII

Nature, indeed, the plot you spin's so stale,
And each man's story is so like another,
I should advise—it's such a boring tale,
Suppress all copies and begin some other.

XLIII

From your sunny clime
Dream of earthly time
And the chill mist,
Wonder at earth's wreck
And the sorrow-strewn deck,
By friend death unkist.

Sailing as for joy,
Happy girl and boy,
In these waters grim
Watch their faces pale,
The broken sail,
For an idle whim.
God's dream, God's whim.

XLIV

Now think how high a mountain is,
Joy, could this tall oak's branches kiss
Its shoulder, less its brow, how blest?
If I lie low the skies are drest
With its broidered branches stretched
    across
Into the sky-scorned mountain's loss,
The sky, it gibbers to forever.
Naught is too low to make so high
As hope, if we stand right, and sever
Waste, the essential to descry.

XLV

Violet is the maddest colour I know
And opal is the colour of dreams,
But a girl is the colour of snow,
The violet like noon haze she seems
And of opal the lights on her brow.

XLVI

Drowsed in beauty
Of her face
Waking fancies
Strive to chase.

XLVII

In the moon's dark fantasy
Here is a woman weeping,
Having the night for a palace.
And here in a house of stone
Harlots feast and revel.

1914

XLVIII

Under these skies, that take the hues
Of metals locked beneath earth,
According as the spirit woos
What changing mood to birth.
Delicate silver gleaming
In threads of tender thought;
Gold in a proud dreaming
Our dream ships have brought;
But the skies of lead
When our hearts are dead,
And the skies relentless
Of an iron petal scentless,
That brooding like a shadow
Weighs down the sunless meadow.

XLIX

All pleasures die,
O clinging lights
And wavering glory,
Adieu you sigh,
Half-told your story,
To you we die.

And like the artist who creates
From dying things what never dies . . .

For one thrilled instant am I you, O skies.
It passes, I am hunted, and the air
Lives with revengeful momentary fires.
O wilderness of heaven,
Whose profound spaces like some God's blank
    eyes
Roll in a milky terror, move and move,
While our fears make vague shuddering imprints
    there
And character such chained-up forms of sorrow
That a breath can unloose; in its white depths
Dream unnamed gulfs of sudden traps for men.
For all men's thoughts go up and form one soul
With unimagined might of evil scheming,
Wrought by the texture of selfish desires,
Of puny plotting, and inspired dreaming.

Or if a thought like spray by sudden moon
Is lit, that holy amorous instant knows
Transplanted time to make twin time in space,
My new-born thought touch aeon-dusted thoughts.
From softly lidded lights, from breaking gleams,
Into a rainbow radiance, some pale light springs,
And the dim Sun stands midwife to this child.

LII

THE SEARCH

Dawn like a flushed rose petal fleck'd with gold
Quickened youth's glow.   Upon my barb I leap'd
While the blank desert's stretchèd leaguers slept,
And loosed his bridle of flame from idling cold.

LIII

Be the hope or the fear,
Be the smile or the tear,
In the strife of a life
On Time's rolling river
That rolls on forever.

LIV

WILD UNDERTONES

I wash my soul in colours, in a million undertones,
And then my soul shines out—and you read—a poem.

LV

I have pressed my teeth in the heart of May,
I have dabbled my lips in the honey of June,
And the sun shot keen and the grass laughed gay
And the earth was buoyed on the tide of noon.

LVI

What songs do fill the pauses of our day
When action tires and motion begs to stay
And life can give to life a little heed?
Then when life only seems to pause
A life divine from heaven she draws,
From labour's earthly trammels freed.

LVII

In dimpled depths of smiling innocence,
In dimpled labyrinths of innocence,
My sunless sorrow made its rosy grave
In laughing liquid eyes that Time had
    wardened.
Fifteen skyey years—my sad soul looked,
My sad soul looked and all its sadness
    vanished.

LVIII

'WHAT MAY BE, WHAT HATH BEEN, AND WHAT IS NOW?'

I said, I have been having some fits of despondency lately; this is what they generally end in, some Byronic sublimity of plaintive caterwauling:

What may be, what hath been, and what is now?
God!   God! if thou art pity, look on me;
God! if thou art forgiveness, turn and see
The dark within, the anguish on my brow!
O! wherefore am I stricken in grief thus low?
For no wrong done, or right undone to thee?
For, if that thou has made me, what must be
Thou hast made too.   How canst thou be thy foe
To retribute what thou thyself hast done?
A little pity, or if that be vain,
If tears are dumb since there to hear are none,
If that the years mean lingering hours of pain,
If rest alone through death's gate is but won,

LIX

The grasses tremble and quiver
Now at the set of day
The host of colours come
In gorgeous disarray

232

LX

SUMMER IN WINTER
SIX THOUGHTS

Before the winter's over
I know a way
The summer to recover,
The August and the May.

Before the month of blossoms
And sunny days,
I know that which unbosoms
Whate'er the summer says.

Ah! would you net the season?
And chain the sun?
For you will flowers do treason?
And how is treason done?

While still the land lies gleaming
And bare and dumb,
And love asleep is dreaming
Of the warm nights to come,

Catch these sweet thoughts in
    shadow,
Bring them to light,
At once the fragrant meadow
Will flash on sense and sight.

Six names of six sweet maidens,
Six honey flowers,
Name, and each name unladens
Its load of summer hours.

Ruth, joyous as a July
Song-throbbing noon,
And rosy as a newly
Flushed eager rose in June.

The August's dreamy languor
Is Maisy sweet.
Drowsed summer when she's sang
     her
Rich songs and rests her feet.

The stately smile and gracious
Of an April wood
    .   .   .   .
Is tall and fair Gertrude.

And like a clear May morning
When birds call clear
And quickly to each other,
Is little Lily dear.

And ripe as buxom Autumn
When she holds hands
With August, fruit enwroughten,
Fair sumptuous Ethel stands.

Sweet gleams of dawn and twilight,
Sunshine in shade,
Is Lena calm as starlight.
Now the six thoughts are said.

LXI

L—— AND M——

Once on a time in a land so fair
That the air you breathed was as wine,
And everything that you looked on there
Made you at once divine,

There lived two maidens, little and sweet,
Whose dear names I may not tell
Because they would call me blab and cheat,
Which would be terrible.

The eldest whom I will just call L,
Was most ladylike and smart,
And of M the youngest, she had ways that—
    well,
One had to guard one's heart.

And in this land, as of course you'd guess,
They did not live all alone,
And all the blessings that God could bless
These two could call their own.

A mother, so wise and good and kind,
A father as young as they
In heart, who while he formed their mind,
He did not mind their play.

They were taught music, and painting, and all
Of culture's thousand pothers,
To dance and to ply the bat and ball,
And also feel for others.

But sad to say, most sad it should be,
They were not always good;
Although they looked so fairily,
They oft did what no fairy would.

When they were set to drawing flowers
Then Lily in pique would say,
'I hate drawing, especially flowers,
Let's throw the flowers away'.

And Maisy, that buxom rosy Miss,
Would set the teacher riddles,
And his brain with 'Can you solve this
    and this?'
Buzzed as if with a hundred fiddles.

INDEX OF TITLES